THE MOST INCREDIBLE EXPLORATION STORIES EVER TOLD

A COLLECTION OF EXTRAORDINARY TALES
FROM OUR WORLD'S GREATEST EXPLORERS

JONATHAN HUNT

ISBN: 979-8-89095-011-6

TABLE OF CONTENTS

ATTENTION:

DO YOU WANT MY FUTURE BOOKS AT HEAVY DISCOUNTS AND EVEN FOR FREE?

HEAD OVER TO WWW.SECRETREADS.COM AND JOIN MY SECRET BOOK CLUB!

INTRODUCTION

We live in a world where we can fly around the world in less than 48 hours.

But as little as a hundred years ago, to journey virtually anywhere in the world was a long, tedious (and dangerous) undertaking.

In what became known as the Age of Exploration, men risked (and sometimes gave) everything to chart unexplored regions around the globe.

These men braved expansive oceans, vast deserts, thick jungles, towering mountains, deadly illnesses, hostile enemy forces, and more…, all in the name of discovery and the pure thrill of adventure.

The Most Incredible Exploration Stories Ever Told reveals to you the exploits of ten famous explorers and the adventures they undertook. Few endeavors have captured the imagination and spirit of humanity as profoundly as exploration. From

1

the earliest wanderings of ancient nomads to the grand expeditions of intrepid navigators, explorers have pushed the boundaries of human knowledge, opening up new frontiers, and connecting cultures across vast distances. In this book, we embark on a captivating journey through time and space to unravel the remarkable tales of some of the greatest explorers the world has ever known.

Spanning continents and centuries, our journey in this book takes us to the distant realms of our world. We will cover Marco Polo, whose travels along the Silk Road unveiled the riches of the East to the astonished West and helped forge an impenetrable bond between Europe and Asia. We follow in the footsteps of David Livingstone, who ventured deep into the heart of Africa, driven by a passion to uncover its secrets and end the Arab-African slave trade.

We sail alongside the famous Christopher Columbus, whose voyage to find a westward route to Asia led to the discovery of the New World..., and who also may have been a part of a deeper strategy that completely changed history as we know it. We also trace the voyages of Amerigo Vespucci, whose keen observations gave a name to the vast landmass that is now known as the Americas, forever immortalizing his contribution to the exploration of the world - except, as we will explore, perhaps it was not America that was named after Amerigo but rather Amerigo who was named after America.

We will also travel north to the frigid wasteland of the Arctic, where we will cover Robert Peary on his relentless quest to reach the North Pole, a dream that finally became a reality. The wilderness of Antarctica on the opposite end of the world was no less forgiving, where the legendary Ernest Shackleton braved unimaginable hardships to lead his men through a tale of survival and heroism that transcends the bounds of human endurance.

Navigating uncharted waters, we will also travel the world and follow the exploits of James Cook, the great British explorer whose voyages mapped vast expanses of the Pacific, Australia, New Zealand, Newfoundland, and Antarctica, forever changing our understanding of the world.

Beyond their names and accomplishments, these explorers were driven by an insatiable curiosity, an unquenchable thirst for discovery that compelled them to face untold dangers and unimaginable hardships. As we peel back these critical and yet overlooked layers of history, we uncover not only their triumphs but also the complexities of their motivations, the impact of their encounters with other cultures, and the lasting legacy of their expeditions.

In this book, we not only celebrate these explorers and adventures and their incredible feats but also delve into the context of their times and the far-reaching consequences of their explorations. We aim to understand how their actions have shaped the world we inhabit today and the lessons we can glean from their remarkable journeys.

It was a vastly different time back then when we didn't know our own world and when to journey anywhere unknown was almost a guaranteed death sentence.

But as we'll also discover, there are still several regions around the world that remain unexplored to this day. Despite all the advances in technology in the last century, the Age of Exploration is perhaps far from over....

MARCO POLO
AND KUBLAI KHAN

The Venetian explorer Marco Polo became famous worldwide for becoming one of the first Europeans to explore vast swaths of Asia, including the Gobi Desert, India, and Tibet. In the process, he met with the fearsome Kublai Khan, grandson of Genghis, but managed to befriend him and serve as his envoy to Europe and other lands. This is their story.

Many years before Christopher Columbus sailed the ocean blue in 1492 or Ferdinand Magellan led a voyage that circumnavigated the globe, another explorer made a name for himself as an explorer - not via sailing but by traveling on land. That explorer was Marco Polo.

It was a vastly different world back then, not only in terms of technology but also the kinds of beliefs held around the world. For instance, many back then believed that the Sun was revolving around the Earth, and not the other way around.

The Silk Road (or more appropriately the Silk Routes) was a series of trade routes connecting Europe to Asia and facilitated trade and commerce between the two regions. The routes, which were nearly 4,000 miles in length, were so-named for the silk textiles that originated in China. Other goods that were commonly traded between Europe and Asia included perfume, dyes, tea, camels, horses, gold, and wine.

Venice served as the epicenter of trade with Asia because much of the goods that came into Europe first came through the Venetian port. Venetian ships would dock at eastern Mediterranean ports in the Middle East, receive the goods, ship them back to Venice, and then distribute them to other European merchants.

The Silk Roads were not just long and complex, they were also incredibly dangerous. Travelers would need to cross over vast deserts and towering mountains to go to and from China. The act of trading goods was no laughing matter and involved long and harrowing journeys that claimed many lives.

This was the world that Marco Polo was born into in 1254. Most historians believe he was born in Venice, right in the middle of trade between Europe and Asia. His was a merchant family, but his father Niccolò and his uncle

Maffeo were away on a long expedition trading while Marco was a child.

While Marco was being raised by his mother and other relatives back home, Niccolò was on his way to China gaining an audience with Kublai Khan. Kublai was the grandson of Genghis Khan who had founded the vast Mongol empire across China. Niccolò and Kublai Khan developed a good working relationship, with the Khan learning much about the European political, economic, and religious systems from Niccolò.

Niccolò did not even know that a son had been born to him while he was away on his journey. When Niccolò finally made it back to Venice, he discovered that he now had a 15-year-old son and that his wife had passed away in his absence.

Niccolò wouldn't stay in Venice for long. Two years later, he left the city again with his brother Maffeo and the now 17-year-old Marco. Niccolò needed to return to Kublai Khan to bring him two specific gifts that he had requested: documents from the Pope and Holy Oil from Jerusalem.

****

Kublai Khan had spent his life building upon what his grandfather Genghis had already started. Kublai effectively ruled over all of what is now Mongolia, China, and Korea. He represented what was easily the greatest known power outside of Europe.

In 1271, Kublai established the Yuan Dynasty and declared Dadu (which is today known as Beijing) as its capital. Kublai focused extensively on modernizing his empire. He ordered the construction of a highway system throughout his lands to facilitate easier travel and trading, constructed many public buildings, introduced a paper currency known as the Jiao Chao (which was hedged against gold and silver as protection against inflation), and also advocated religious and cultural tolerance throughout the Mongolian Empire.

As an example of his tolerance, Kublai was personally very opposed to Daoism, (a.k.a Taoism) and yet he ordered that all Taoist temples be preserved, and Taos be free to practice their religion. He was also opposed to Islam, and yet had many Muslims in his court.

During his meeting with Niccolò Polo, Kublai granted him a gold passport that permitted Niccolò and his brother to use horses and houses that were controlled by the Mongols along the Silk Road. This was crucial because traveling the Silk Road across the vast expanse of Asia and back to Kublai in Dadu took over three years to complete. The horses and lodging provided by the Mongols enroute helped ensure the safety of Niccolò, Maffeo, and Marco as they traveled.

The Polo entourage finally reached Kublai again in 1275, and Niccolò presented Marco to the Khan. Enroute, Niccolò ensured that Marco was properly educated in learning the Mongolian language, so Marco and Kublai were able to openly communicate with one another.

Kublai was eager to work with non-Mongolian individuals who could serve in diplomatic and administrative roles facilitating communication between his capital of Dadu with the European powers to the west. This was why Kublai had many Muslims in his court already to facilitate such communication with the Islamic nations in Arabia and the Middle East.

Marco found great favor with Kublai, who found the young Venetian to be well-spoken, intelligent, and respectful. Kublai assigned Marco to serve as his emissary to Burma and India, and he dispatched Marco on many diplomatic endeavors throughout the Mongol Empire and the Orient.

As a result of these missions, Marco was able to explore many areas of Asia such as Indonesia, Vietnam, and Sri Lanka. Many lands that Marco explored had previously not been known to Europeans.

Marco would always return to Kublai and use his storytelling skills to describe all that he had witnessed on these missions. Kublai greatly appreciated the Polos both for their company and for their usefulness in ensuring diplomacy throughout his empire. In fact, he loved having the Polos in his service so much that he denied their repeated requests to return home. This goes to show how Kublai Khan saw the Polos more as his subjects rather than as merely friends or emissaries.

However, in 1291 Kublai finally relented and granted the Polos their request to return home. However, even the return home was to be yet another diplomatic mission for the Khan, as he wanted the Polos to accompany the Mongolian princess Kokochin to Persia to become the new wife of Arghun Khan.

When Marco Polo finally returned home to Venice in 1295, he was 41 years old, having spent 24 years of his life abroad throughout Asia. During this time, he and his father and uncle had covered almost 15,000 miles of ground, an incredible feat.

****

The Polos were also now very wealthy people. Marco had his wealth converted into gemstones, and also used part of it to convert a galley into a warship to help the Venetians in their war against the Genoans, another maritime Italian city-state.

Marco was captured by the Genoans in a battle somewhere off the Anatolian coast, and he would spend the next several months of his life in a Genoan prison. This would turn out to be a crucial turning point in making his later global exploits famous.

While in prison, Marco met another man named Rustichello da Pisa and recounted the stories of his adventures in Asia to him. Da Pisa wrote all of Marco's detailed exploits down on paper, and eventually created a full manuscript called *The Million*; so-titled because it was Marco's nickname. The work was eventually renamed *The Travels of Marco Polo* and told the story of Marco's journey with his father and uncle to see Kublai Khan, his service as a diplomat in the service of the Khan, and his adventures throughout India, China, and Japan.

The work was significant because it unveiled much about Asia that was previously unknown to Europeans, including descriptions of previously unknown wildlife as well as covering the political, economic, and religious spheres of the region.

Marco remained imprisoned until late 1299. After that he returned home to Venice where he reunited with his father and uncle and purchased a large palace, or palazzo, using the gemstones that they had converted from their time in the East. The trio developed a successful merchant company and financed several more expeditions into Asia and the Silk Road. However, neither Marco nor his father and uncle ever returned to Asia again.

In 1300, Marco's father Niccolò passed away, and he married the daughter of a merchant named Fantina, with whom he had three daughters. Marco continued to live the life of a successful Venetian merchant until his own death in 1324. Due to the Venetian law stating that the day ends at sunset, the exact date of Marco Polo's death cannot be determined, but according to some scholars it was between the sunsets of 8 and 9 January 1324.

****

The exploits of Marco Polo are notable because of how instrumental he and his father and uncle were in helping forge a dialogue and understanding between East and West. Thanks to the efforts of Marco and his father and brother, both East and West learned much about the religious, political, and cultural views of the other.

However, Marco Polo would have likely been completely forgotten had it not been for da Pisa's successful book. Back then, printing did not exist, so, there were only around a hundred or more handwritten manuscripts across several different languages of the work in existence.

But enough copies of da Pisa's book survived, and when printing was invented a couple of hundred years later, *The Travels of Marco Polo* became famous across Europe. To this day, it is unclear if Polo or da Pisa wrote the book. Some scholars believe both men made contributions, as part of the book is in the first person and other parts are in the third person. Scholars also argue about whether or not Polo exaggerated his exploits in the book to make himself appear more favorable.

What's undeniable, however, is that the work was historically accurate and helped provide valuable insights into Asian customs, traditions, and economics. For instance, the work introduced the idea of paper money to the

Europeans, as well as the idea of burning coal for use as heat.

The Travels of Marco Polo became so successful that it inspired several other Europeans to embark on their own journeys of exploration. Christopher Columbus in particular was so impressed by the work that he carried a copy of it with him on his journey west across the Atlantic.

Polo's family also created several maps that were based on Polo's detailed descriptions. Polo's three daughters (Fantina, Moreta, and Bellela) produced detailed maps of China, Russia, Japan, and even Alaska. This was almost a full two centuries before Columbus would sail to the Americas, which disrupts the traditional narrative that Columbus was the first European to discover the so-called "New World."

Marco Polo was one of the most instrumental explorers in human history. Not only did he help to bridge the gap that existed between Europe and the Asian nations to the East, but his exploits also motivated many other explorers to go searching into the great unknown. This helped to set the foundation for the "Age of Exploration" as it came to be called, in the upcoming years.

VASCO DA GAMA
AND HIS JOURNEY
ACROSS THE WORLD

In the late 1400s, at the peak of the Age of Exploration, famed Portuguese explorer Vasco da Gama led his crew on a 24,000-mile voyage around the world to try to chart a trading route to the East. The harrowing trip involved deadly scurvy outbreaks and violent encounters with hostile foreign forces along the way, costing the lives of more than half of the crew members.

The Age of Exploration, as we know it today, was perhaps a byproduct of another age: the Age of Sail.

That's because it really was the advent of the sailing ship that made exploration of distant regions of the world possible. This then permitted colonization, which also made possible for expansive trade routes and set the stage for the geopolitical and economic systems of today. Marco Polo may have learnt much by traveling on land, but there were other lands to be explored that were accessible only by ship.

15

While sailing ships had been in existence for thousands of years, most ships from previous eras had been built for expeditions on shorter routes. By the 15th century, European sailing ships had evolved into square rigs that were larger (so they could carry more cargo) and with at least three masts and multiple large sails. These developments permitted them to cover much longer distances over open seas than most ships previously had been capable of sailing.

Many explorers, financed by the monarchs and wealthy businessmen of the day, made names for themselves in this age.

One of these men was named Vasco da Gama.

****

As we'll discuss later in this book, the Spanish primarily moved west to explore the lands beyond the Atlantic. But while the Spanish were out exploring the Americas to the west, the Portuguese turned their attention to the opposite direction.

At that time, there was strong interest in finding a trade route to Southeastern Asia, which was a source of many valuables including spices, silk, and even gold. Since the Portuguese were situated on the far western side of Europe, it was a dangerous (and long) journey to find a new route that could take a ship all the way to the Orient.

To accomplish this mission, they would need to employ the services of a skilled and courageous navigator. Vasco de Gama would become that navigator.

Da Gama was born in either 1460 or 1469 in the coastal town of Sines, Portugal. His father, Estevao, was a prominent member of the military Order of Santiago. Estevao later became integrated into the Military Order of Christ when he married Isabel Sodre, whose father was a member of the order. Vasco was the third of Estevao and Isabel's five sons.

Vasco da Gama's familial connections to the Military Order of Christ are worth mentioning because, as we'll later explore in this book, there was a connection between Christopher Columbus and the Military Order of Christ as well. The Military Order of Christ itself was also significant because it represented part of the remnants of the Knights Templar.

On March 22, 1312, Pope Clement V issued a papal bull ordering the abolishment and the capture of the Templars under pressure from King Philip IV of France, who was deeply in debt to their order. While most of the Templars were wiped out (either dying in prison or facing horrific public executions), several members managed to evade capture and sought protection in other lands.

Some found refuge in Scotland (like we'll also discuss in this book later), but many others found safety in Portugal, where King Diniz refused to persecute the former knights. Scotland and Portugal both essentially became safe havens for Templar survivors and for those who were sympathetic to their cause.

Diniz even went so far as to revive the Templar order, doing so under another name: the Military Order of Christ. Members of the Military Order of Christ proved consequential to the Reconquista when the Iberian Peninsula was reclaimed from the Islamic Moors.

And also, like Columbus, there exists very little information about da Gama's early life.

It is believed that he studied navigation at Evora, and it is possible he may have studied astrology and astronomy as well.

In 1480, da Gama followed in the footsteps of his father Estevao to join the Military Order of Christ. The King of

Portugal at that time was John II, who like King Diniz from over a hundred years ago, heavily supported the Order. The educated and capable da Gama gained the attention of John II, who selected him to seize French ships at Algarve (the southernmost region of Portugal). Da Gama commanded the task with ease and ahead of schedule, further winning the favor of the monarch.

By now, the Portuguese Age of Exploration was in full swing. Under Prince Henry the Navigator, the Portuguese had been sailing down the western African coastline in search of gold and slaves (two of the most valuable commodities at the time) over the last several decades. While these expeditions did much to expand Portuguese knowledge of Africa, they were not very profitable.

It was for this reason that the Portuguese nobility was not particularly eager to finance further explorations. John II, however, had shown an intense interest in exploration even before he officially ascended to the throne. Unlike other members of the nobility, John II believed that great riches could be accumulated for the Portuguese crown via Africa.

John II also believed that Portugal could take part in the spice trade that existed between Asia and Europe, which at that time was being facilitated by the Republic of Venice primarily via land (with Egypt and the Levant serving as the gateway into Asia) rather than by sea.

Upon ascending to the throne in 1481, John II immediately put into effect new reforms. He ordered Portuguese expeditions along the West African coast to resume, and he also decreed a new task: to discover a sea route to the Orient by sailing around the African continent. John II believed that if the Portuguese could find a new naval route to the Orient, it would allow them to compete effectively with the Venetians.

In 1488, John II dispatched Captain Bartolomeu Dias, who rounded the Cape of Good Hope and was able to confirm that the continent continued to stretch to the northeast. But another explorer would be needed who could build upon what Dias had accomplished and find a trade route that would continue from the Cape of Good Hope and go all the way to India and the Orient.

Even though John II passed away in 1495, his successor King Manuel I decided to build upon his predecessor's legacy and continue to sponsor expeditions in an attempt to find a naval route to the Orient. The man selected for the mission was the same young talented man who had impressed John II on the mission to seize the French ships at Algarve years earlier: da Gama.

Da Gama was provided with a fleet of four ships to be crewed by 170 men. A handful of these men were among the most experienced and skilled navigators Portugal had at the time, including Pedro Escobar and Pero de Alenquer. The four ships under da Gama's command were the *Sao Gabriel, Sao Rafael, San Miguel,* and a fourth storage ship.

Upon his official dispatched from Lisbon on 8 July 1497, little did da Gama know that his upcoming voyage would cover a distance greater than the entire length of the equator.

Da Gama initially followed the routes that had been established by earlier Portuguese explorers by moving along the coast of Africa and the Cape Verde and Tenerife Islands. He later followed Dias's course through the westerly winds in the South Atlantic. On November 4, da Gama's fleet was able to reach the African coast. They then rounded the Cape of Good Hope on the southern coast of Africa and reached the Great Fish River, which was where Dias had formally stopped.

Da Gama's fleet had already crossed over 6,000 miles of ocean, which was the longest by far recorded journey conducted by Europeans at that time, and now they were about to embark into waters that had been unknown to them up until that time. Before leaving the Great Fish River, da Gama and his crew named the region "Natal," meaning the "Birth of Christ" in Portuguese. This region in eastern South Africa still carries this name to this day.

Da Gama and his crew now traveled up the eastern side of Africa, going along the coast of what is now Mozambique, with only three ships as the fourth storage ship was scuttled. They were now about to enter Arab-controlled territory. Knowing that the local population would be friendly to Muslims but potentially hostile to Christians, da Gama pretended to be a Muslim when he met with the Sultan of Mozambique. The meeting went very poorly, as the Sultan was unimpressed with the gifts da Gama had to offer. Da Gama and his men barely escaped with their lives back to the ships, and da Gama even ordered the cannons to fire back into the coastal town.

Da Gama's expedition continued up the eastern African coast into what is now Tanzania and Kenya. Running low on supplies, da Gama and his crew were forced to turn to loot unarmed Arab merchant trading ships. Da Gama sailed into Mombasa, but as in Mozambique, they were met with hostility and sailed away not long after they arrived.

Continuing up the Kenyan coastline, da Gama's crew now reached the port of Malindi. The people there were engaged in an armed conflict with Mombasa. Here da Gama was at long last able to gain a friendlier reception and gained knowledge from the residents about the monsoon winds that could take them to Calicut on the coast of India.

Da Gama followed his newly provided route across the Indian ocean, and the fleet arrived at the Malabar Coast in what is now southwestern India. Da Gama sought an audience with the local Zamorin (or King), but his gifts failed to impress. The Zamorin only wanted gold or silver, which da Gama did not provide.

Da Gama left Calicut and worked his way slowly up the Indian coastline before deciding to return home. But whereas crossing the Indian Ocean before had only taken just over 20 days, the return trip took over 132 days because he was forced to sail against the wind. But the slow return was not the only affliction upon the crew. Scurvy broke out and over half of the crew perished before catching sight of land again.

Finally, da Gama's fleet caught sight of land again - what is now Somalia in the Horn of Africa. Encouraged, the survivors continued down to the African coast and back to the friendly port of Malindi. Since da Gama no longer had enough men to run three ships. Da Gama then ordered *Sao Rafael* to be scuttled, with *Sao Gabriel* and *San Miguel* the only two vessels remaining in his fleet.

After enough of his crew had recovered from scurvy, da Gama resumed the journey home. They followed the way back that they had originally come, going back around the Cape of Good Hope and continuing back up the West African coast.

Upon da Gama's arrival back in Portugal, the news of the expedition's results was met with a mixed reaction. On one hand, da Gama had established a route for circling the southern tip of Africa and continuing to Asia, and he had also returned with many spices and trade goods. But the expedition had been completed at a massive cost with the loss of two ships and more than half of the crew, and furthermore, da Gama had failed in his principal mission of establishing a successful trading relationship with the leaders in India.

Nonetheless, the voyage provided proof that a seafaring route was made possible for establishing trade with Asia and this would prove vital to Portuguese interests in the upcoming decades.

****

Da Gama's voyage was hardly the first he would take, but in the meantime, he would spend the next several years in Portugal. He was rewarded for his actions by being granted the town of Sines by the crown, but he would spend several years attempting to claim it when the Master of the Order of Santiago (Jorge de Lencastre) refused to grant Da Gama the city. He was also provided with a substantial annual pension and granted several noble titles. Da Gama married into the powerful Almedia family when he married Catarina de Ataide in 1501.

War broke out in 1500 between Portugal and Calicut. The Portuguese had sent another fleet there and attempted to establish a factory, but when violent conflict erupted (with both sides blaming the other), da Gama used his royal titles to take command of the 4th India Armada, consisting of 15 warships and 800 men at arms.

Da Gama then set sail back to India in February 1502 with his cousin Estavao commanding five more ships as reinforcements. It was at this point that da Gama began to display a particularly brutal and merciless streak to his character, which was perhaps fueled by his desire for revenge against the Zamorin from their prior encounter.

The fleet arrived in Calicut in October of that year, but not before da Gama had encountered and brutally massacred the inhabitants of an Arabian pilgrim ship enroute. Despite the inhabitants of the ship begging for mercy, da Gama ordered the vessel to be set ablaze with everyone still onboard, including women and children. The massacre of these pilgrims on da Gama's orders is considered to be the most notorious incident of his life.

The Zamorin of Calicut had received word of the slaughter before da Gama arrived, and while he acted very peacefully at the return of the Portuguese he refused da Gama's demand to remove all Muslims from his kingdom before trade negotiations could be discussed.

Open hostilities broke out between the Indians and the Portuguese yet again. After one of his priests was returned to him with his lips and ears cut off and a pair of dog's ears sewn to the side of his head. Then, da Gama bombarded this unfortified city from afar for two days, the Zamorin resolved to fight back and dispatched a large fleet to engage da Gama.

In the ensuing Battle of Calicut, the Indians were decisively defeated and suffered heavy losses despite their fleet heavily outnumbering da Gama's forces. Da Gama then sought alliances with the rival Indian kingdoms of Cannanore and Cochin, loading up his ships with spices and trade goods in the process.

Having defeated the Zamorin in battle and stocked with spices, da Gama left India in early 1503 to return to Portugal. This time, however, his return was not greeted warmly.

Even though da Gama had defeated the Zamorin's forces in combat and won a military victory for Portugal, he had failed to bring the Zamorin to negotiating terms. This failure overlooked da Gama's success in securing spices from Cannanore and Cochin as well.

As a result, the next several years of da Gama's life were rather quiet and uneventful. He was overlooked for the position of viceroy of India, and he was not invited back to the Royal Court as well for several years.

Da Gama spent the next several years attempting to win back the favor of the Portuguese crown. When news broke out that Ferdinand Magellan (another renowned Portuguese explorer who we'll talk about later in this book) had defected to the Spanish, da Gama threatened to do the same unless he was granted a feudal title.

This put the Portuguese monarchy in a tight bind. Failure to grant da Gama a title would embarrass the monarchy further if he defected, and having him captured or murdered would only turn him into a martyr.

As a result, King Manuel I titled da Gama a 'count', which provided da Gama and his heirs with numerous royal privileges and money. When Manuel I passed away a few years later, he was succeeded by King John III, who held da Gama in much higher regard.

John III even went as far as to make da Gama one of his closest advisors, and he even made da Gama a governor and later viceroy of Portuguese India.

****

Da Gama set sail on his third and final voyage to India in April 1524. This time he had 14 ships at his command, and despite losing five of the vessels enroute, he finally arrived in India in September.

Not long after his arrival, however, da Gama contracted malaria and was unable to recover. He died three months later on Christmas Eve in the city of Cochin in 1524. He was buried there until his remains were returned to Portugal in 1539.

In his lifetime, da Gama gained a reputation as a talented naval commander who was both strong-willed and yet brutal in his dealings with other people, including the natives of the lands he visited. His most notable accomplishment was establishing a seafaring route from western Europe and Asia that went around the Cape of Good Hope. Due to da Gama's discovery, Portugal was able to send more ships and secure outposts across eastern Africa, India, and the Orient.

The Age of Exploration had just begun.

FERDINAND MAGELLAN'S EXPEDITION TO INDONESIA

Vasco de Gama was not the only explorer from Portugal to chart a course around the world. Ferdinand Magellan set sail with four ships under the Spanish banner for Indonesia. He couldn't have known then that the upcoming voyage would cost the lives of over half of the men who set sail…, including his own.

Ferdinand Magellan would chart a course the opposite way around the world that da Gama went. Whereas da Gama sailed around the southern tip of Africa and up into India, Magellan would cross the Atlantic, discover a way across South America, and chart a new course across the endless bounds of the Pacific.

Magellan was born in 1480 in northern Portugal. As with da Gama, there is much that we don't know about his early life, other than that his father was a part of the Portuguese nobility and the mayor of his local town, that he had one brother and one sister, and that from an early age he was involved with the Portuguese monarchy.

This was because Magellan was raised as a page (or royal servant) of the Portuguese queen Eleanor, who was the wife of King John II. When Manuel I became king after the passing of John II, Magellan entered his service.

From an early age, Magellan had a thirst for adventure. In 1505, when Francisco de Almeida commanded a fleet of 22 ships to return to Portuguese India to continue with the negotiations that da Gama had established, Magellan enlisted in the service of the fleet.

He would spend eight years of his life in India, Malaysia, and eastern Africa, during which he fought for the Portuguese in numerous battles (surviving several serious wounds in the process) and learned much about seafaring and navigation, trading and negotiating, and warfare and combat. These years would prove to be instrumental in Magellan's life because, without the experiences and skills he developed during this time, he never would have been able to undertake the future voyage that would make him famous.

Magellan returned to Portugal in 1513. Despite having built a good reputation for himself from his time serving

Portugal overseas, he was accused of illegal trading with the Moors, and while he was later proven innocent in court, the accusations left a permanent stain on his reputation. He was also wounded in battle during an expedition in Morocco, which gave him a limp he would carry for the rest of his life.

Magellan's good friend (and possible cousin) with whom he had served overseas, Francisco Serrao, discovered the Spice Islands (so-named because of the nutmeg and cloves that were found there) in Moluccas, Indonesia. Serrao wrote of his discovery to Magellan, who soon became fascinated with leading an expedition to find a westward route to the Spice Islands (instead of the eastern route around the southern tip of Africa that the Portuguese were currently using).

Magellan submitted several requests to King Manuel I to finance such an expedition but was repeatedly denied. On one hand, Magellan was asking for a substantial sum of money to invest in a high-risk, high-reward voyage that had a high probability of failure, which is perhaps the primary reason why Manuel I denied his request. On the other hand, Magellan's reputation had an irreversible stain from the incident with the Moors, which perhaps sealed

Manuel I's decision to deny Magellan a fleet of ships to carry out the expedition.

Unable to recoup his favor with the Portuguese monarchy, Magellan officially renounced his Portuguese nationality and left for Seville in Spain. Here he married and had two children, and dedicated himself to studying the most updated charts for finding a westward pathway from the Atlantic into the Pacific.

The King of Spain, Charles I, (later emperor Charles V of the Holy Roman Empire) was more receptive to Magellan's ideas when he presented them to the Spanish monarchy. This was largely because of the 1494 Treaty of Tordesillas, which had been created by Pope Alexander as a preemptive means to stop Spain and Portugal from warring with one another.

The treaty granted Portugal access to the eastern routes to Asia around the Cape of Good Hope as Diaz and da Gama had found. The Spanish were granted the westward route to Asia.

Magellan was able to convince Charles I that under the terms of the treaty the Spice Islands would fall under Spanish jurisdiction. He also convinced Charles that he had the necessary experience and skills to chart a westward course to the islands by sailing across the Atlantic and traveling down and around the tip of South America.

Subsequently, Charles I granted Magellan five ships (*Trinidad*, *Victoria*, *Concepcion*, *San Antonio*, and *Santiago*), 270 men, and enough supplies to last for two years of voyaging. The upcoming voyage would be the first recorded in history to completely circumnavigate the globe.

****

Magellan's five-ship fleet departed Seville on August 10, 1519. The ships traveled down the Guadalquivir River before stopping at the Sanlucar de Barrameda at the edge of Spain. The crew waited five more weeks to collect more supplies and make final preparations before finally setting sail into the Atlantic.

The fleet's first stop was in Tenerife in the Canary Islands, where they acquired more supplies. But already, trouble was brewing for the fleet. While staying in Tenerife, Magellan received a message from his father-in-law (Diogo Barbosa) that warned him the Castilian captains on the ships were planning a mutiny led by Juan de Cartagena (captain of the San Antonio) and that King Manuel I had dispatched his own fleet of Portuguese warships to overtake and subdue Magellan.

Magellan now had the Portuguese on his tail and knew he couldn't trust several of his own men, particularly the Spanish members and captains of the crew who were wary of Magellan's Portuguese heritage. These men wondered if Magellan was secretly still loyal to Portugal and planned to sabotage the fleet to embarrass the Spanish crown.

The fleet departed from the Canary Islands and sailed along the African coast, with Magellan and Cartagena repeatedly locking horns over which way to direct the fleet. Magellan favored following the coast of Africa because he believed the Portuguese pursuers were looking for him out in the open ocean.

The fleet finally turned west toward the Americas after reaching the trade winds near the equator. During the crossing, the boatswain of the Victoria (Antonio Salamon) was caught engaging in lewd acts with one of the cabin boys. Homosexuality was illegal in Spain at that time and punishable by death. Magellan subsequently held a trial, which would find Salamon guilty. Magellan then executed him right after the fleet reached Brazil.

Almost immediately after the trial of Salamon, Cartagena made his move and announced that he would no longer follow Magellan's leadership. Magellan, however, had anticipated Cartagena's betrayal based on the note from his father-in-law and had several armed men arrest Cartagena. Seeing this, the other Castilian captains decided not to back up Cartagena.

Magellan planned to have Cartagena executed as well, but many of the men were very disheartened by the execution of Salamon and the captains pleaded with Magellan to spare Cartagena's life. Magellan relented but relieved Cartagena of command of San Antonio.

In mid-December, the fleet arrived in Rio de Janeiro for some badly needed respite. The crew were exhausted from their long journey across the Atlantic and low on supplies, but the time they spent in Rio did much to restock their resources and renew their spirits. Even though Rio was normally Portuguese-held territory, there were no signs of Portuguese vessels or settlements there, so Magellan and his men knew it would be safe to wade ashore.

The men were warmly received by the indigenous people, who had prophesied that it would rain again when "men from heaven" would come to them. Sure enough, it started raining as Magellan and his men came ashore.

The crew spent nearly two weeks in Rio, during which they resupplied their food and water, repaired their ships, and traded and engaged in sometimes raucous parties with the locals.

After the stop in Rio, Magellan continued the fleet's journey down the eastern coast of South America. The locals at Rio had tried to entice Magellan to stay, but he knew that if the men became too comfortable in Rio, they would never want to continue on their journey to chart the course to the Spice Islands.

In late March, the ship came to the Bay of San Julian in modern-day southern Argentina, where Magellan decided to stop the fleet and prepare for the final trip around South America. However, whispers amongst the crew members continued that Magellan was planning their doom for Portugal's glory.

During Mass on Easter Sunday, the three Spanish captains failed to attend, having conspired to remove Magellan from power and sail the fleet back to Spain. Cartagena and another captain named Luis Mendoza led 30 men aboard

San Antonio, where they took command of the ship. Adding *San Antonio* to *Victoria* and *Concepcion*, Mendoza now commanded three of the five ships in the fleet.

Yet again, though, Magellan was aware of the plot and had his own plan ready to counter the mutineers. Since the ships were anchored in a bay with only one exit to the sea, Magellan knew he could block off the exit with one of his two ships. He deployed *Santiago* for this task.

This meant that Mendoza had no hope of escaping without a fight, and would either have to engage Magellan in battle or negotiate. Mendoza offered to negotiate. When Magellan and his men approached Mendoza, however, they immediately drew their weapons and stabbed Mendoza repeatedly in the neck, killing him.

The rebels were shocked by the abrupt and unexpected act of violence and immediately swore their allegiance to Magellan again. Magellan granted mercy to most of the rebels because he knew that he would need them to continue to run the fleet, but he subjected the rebels to hard labor and marooned several of the leaders on a deserted island, including Cartagena.

Magellan's actions, while harsh, re-established himself as the undisputed leader of the expedition. For the remainder of the voyage, he made sure that most of the hard physical labor was completed by the men who had rebelled against him.

By now, supplies were running dangerously low. Magellan dispatched one ship, *Santiago*, to move ahead to find straits to the Pacific Ocean. Instead, *Santiago* sailed right into the middle of a storm and was wrecked along the coast. The surviving crew members had to hike back up the coastline to the fleet, which was spending its time restocking supplies and interacting with the Tehuelche natives, who were also friendly.

Magellan waited until the middle of October, when the seas became calmer, to continue the voyage. Eventually, the fleet came across a strait, which Magellan sailed into. Unbeknownst to him, this strait would one day bear his name and continue to bear it to this day.

While the straits were hard to navigate due to the sometimes dangerously shallow water and brutal storms, they crossed across the continent to the Pacific. Along the way, the crew was left awestruck by the massive glaciers and fires caused by lightning that they viewed along the way.

It took over a month for the fleet to cross the straits into the Pacific, only for another mutiny to strike.

****

Magellan woke up one morning to find that the crew of *San Antonio* had left with the ship. This was a major blow because *San Antonio* effectively served as the fleet's supply ship. When it arrived back in Seville in May of that year, the crew bad-mouthed Magellan.

As for the last three ships, *Trinidad*, *Concepcion*, and *Victoria*, they were in for a much longer remaining portion of the voyage than Magellan had anticipated. Magellan believed that the journey to the Spice Islands was by now almost complete, but they were about to embark on the largest part of the voyage yet across the world's biggest ocean.

For three whole months, Magellan's fleet was at sea in desperate search of land. This was the toughest time of the journey yet, as many of the men became ill with scurvy, and food and water supplies ran dangerously low. The men were reduced to eating biscuits that were filled with worms and stained with rat urine.

Dozens of men perished from scurvy or starvation. Magellan ensured that the higher-quality food (with appropriate levels of Vitamin C to counter scurvy) and water were reserved for himself and his officers, which meant they did not become afflicted with scurvy even though most of the men were suffering heavily.

It wasn't until February that the crew caught sight of land when they sailed past the islands of Micronesia, but to their exasperation, they were unable to make landfall because of the coral reefs. Furthermore, the islands did not match the description of the Spice Islands either. Magellan became so infuriated that he threw all of his maps and charts into the ocean.

Then, on March 6, the fleet finally caught sight of land again and made landfall on Guam in the Marianas Islands. This was to the immense relief of the surviving crew, as they were running dangerously low on supplies and had become utterly exhausted from nearly 100 days of nonstop sea travel.

The residents of Guam were also friendly and provided the survivors who came ashore with fresh water and food.

Rejuvenated, Magellan and his crew continued on a few weeks later, eventually coming to the Philippines and landing on the island of Cebu. Yet again, the inhabitants were very friendly and welcoming and provided fresh water and food. This lifted their spirits and provided them with badly needed nourishment.

Magellan had crossed the Atlantic, discovered a straight that cut across South America into the Pacific, and then crossed the Pacific to the Philippines. But he still wasn't satisfied even though he had already done the impossible.

He had lost two ships and dozens of men along the way, but now he was absolutely adamant that the Spice Islands couldn't be far away. In reality, they were still over a thousand miles away.

And little did Magellan know; the Philippines would be his last stop.

****

As it turned out, Magellan would never find the Spice Islands, as he got caught in the middle of a violent struggle between two opposing native factions in Cebu.

Magellan had befriended the local rajah, or king, of Cebu. He even succeeded in baptizing the Rajah and his wife into the Catholic faith. He gave them the Christian names of Carlos and Juana in honor of King Charles and also provided a Mass service for them.

The Rajah then ordered all of the local chiefs in the area to convert to Christianity as well. While most of the chiefs followed, one of the chiefs from the island of Mactan refused. This chief in particular, whose name was Datu Lapulapu, had long been rebellious to the Rajah. Magellan saw an opportunity because he knew if he could subdue Lapulapu, it would strengthen the alliance with the Rajah even further.

Magellan then traveled to Mactan with 60 men-at-arms. There he was greeted by a force of no less than 15,000 warriors commanded by Lapulapu.

As the Europeans came ashore, led by Magellan, they found themselves attacked by the full weight of Lapulapu's force. Lapulapu had divided his army into three divisions of around 500 men each to attack the Europeans from the front and both flanks.

Despite being hugely outnumbered, Magellan's men were heavily clad in armor, which protected them from the stones and bamboo spears of Lapulapu's men. Several musketeers and crossbowmen on the boats also fired into Lapulapu's force to inflict casualties and help keep them at bay.

Magellan's overconfidence was about to be his undoing. He ordered his men to continue to press onward to the houses that he could see beyond the beach. The men set fire to the houses while continuing to fight Lapulapu's men.

Then, a poisoned arrow fired from one of the natives flew through the air and struck Magellan in an unarmored part of his leg in the thick of the combat. Several warriors then charged forward to engage Magellan, recognizing him as the leader of the attack and eager to take him down. Magellan was struck again and again by spears and bladed weapons, and while his armor protected him from a majority of the blows, several blades found their mark in the unprotected areas of his limbs.

Magellan's men were unable to help him. They were being attacked by dozens of warriors themselves and were slowly forced back to the sea where they were forced to finally abandon the fight and rejoin the boats.

The last they saw of Magellan he was fighting valiantly but hopelessly against dozens of warriors who were attacking and striking at him with their weapons from all sides.

****

After the death of Magellan, the Rajah turned on the sailors. He had several of Magellan's men poisoned during a feast, at which point the surviving men reboarded *Trinidad* and *Victoria* and promptly left Cebu.

The surviving crew, consisting of around 60 men, would go on to accomplish Magellan's dream. Down to only two ships, after *Conception* was burned and abandoned, the fleet pressed on until they caught the smell of cinnamon and cloves in the air. Following the smell, the ships eventually came to Tidore in the Spice Islands.

The primary goal of the voyage was at long last complete, and Magellan had been correct all along. There indeed was a route for traveling westward and around South America to reach the Spice Islands.

The men loaded up the ships with all the spices they could find, trading metal tools, bells, cloth, and glass to the natives.

During their time in Indonesia, the men also encountered Asian junk ships, elephants, and other flora and fauna native to southeastern Asia.

Having accomplished its goal of charting the westward route to the Spice Islands, the voyage now had only one mission left: to return home.

Trinidad was abandoned in Indonesia as it was leaking too badly to continue, so *Victoria* sailed from Timor and crossed the Indian Ocean to the Cape of Good Hope. From there, it sailed up the African coast before reaching the Cape Verde islands and proceeding from there after resupply.

In early September of 1522, *Victoria* finally reached Spain again.

Only 18 men were left.

****

Magellan's voyage had sailed 60,000 miles and completely circumnavigated the globe. The voyage left Seville in Spain, crossed the Atlantic, crossed South America in the later-to-be-named 'Strait of Magellan', crossed the Pacific, found the Spice Islands, crossed the Indian Ocean, rounded the Cape of Good Hope, and journeyed up the western African coastline back to Seville where it had originally started.

The voyage brought back immense volumes of spices, which the Spanish monarchy was able to sell and trade for great profit, proving to ultimately be a successful investment for the Spanish monarchy.

The voyage also cost the lives of over 250 members of the crew and four of the five ships. The 18 survivors spoke poorly of Magellan upon their return, as many of them were men who had participated in the mutinies before.

As a result, Magellan was largely reviled across both Spain and Portugal. It wasn't until a few years later that historians began to credit Magellan for having started what was perhaps the greatest sea voyage the world had ever known.

Subsequently, several other voyages were dispatched in an attempt to follow Magellan's path and complete a circumnavigation around the world as well. All failed (showing just how lucky the survivors of Magellan's crew really were) until nearly 60 years later when Francis Drake was able to circumnavigate the world in his ship, the Golden Hind.

Magellan is today widely regarded as one of the greatest explorers of all time. In his honor, not only does the Strait of Magellan in southern South America bear his name, but NASA has named a class of its spacecraft after him as well as two dwarf galaxies called the Magellanic Clouds.

Magellan's mission was to find a westward route to the Spice Islands. On top of that, and even in his death, he was able to prove that completely circumnavigating the world was possible. His voyage represented a massive step forward for humanity in its exploration of the world..., an exploration that is still not fully completed to this day.

AMERICA...OR WAS CHRISTOPHER COLUMBUS THE FIRST EUROPEAN TO?

Christopher Columbus is world renowned for being the first European to cross the Atlantic and land in America...or was he? More evidence that has recently come to light in North America casts doubt on this fact, and the true meaning behind Columbus's unique signature that he included in his letters also hints at a potentially hidden reason for his voyage. There may have been more to Columbus than initially meets the eye.

Who was Christopher Columbus?

Almost everyone hears the name and associates it with the European discovery of the Americas, and yet far fewer people can probably tell you who exactly Christopher Columbus was.

That's because we really don't know who he was. Columbus's early life is obscure, but scholars believe he was born in the Republic of Genoa between 25 August and 31 October 1451. Others claim that Columbus was in reality a Greek prince and that his name was merely a cover, while others claim that he was really from Sardinia or Poland.

What is much more well-known is the state of European exploration at the time of Columbus. The Silk Road had long provided Europeans with a consistent (if long and also sometimes unsafe) passage route to China and eastern Asia, which were sources of very valuable trade goods. The efforts of Marco Polo and his father and uncle helped to bridge the gap that existed between Europe and Asia as well in terms of the cultural and economic understanding between the two regions.

But on May 29, 1453, Constantinople fell to the Islamic Ottoman Empire, which also gave them access to most of the entry points to the Silk Road. The Ottomans then closed off this route to the Europeans, giving them a monopoly on trade with China and other Asian countries.

This is why European countries were now forced to find seafaring routes to get to Asia instead. As early as the 1470s, the idea of sailing west across the Atlantic to get to the Indies and eastern Asia had been brought up and discussed.

Columbus was publicly proposing ideas to reach the Indies by sailing west as well by the 1480s.

However, in 1488 Bartolomeu Dias had rounded the Cape of Good Hope, which showed that there was a navigable passage to Asia. As we discussed earlier in this book, this passage would later be furthered by Vasco da Gama when he and his men rounded the Cape of Good Hope as well to reach India.

Columbus was eventually able to gain sponsorship to lead a westward voyage to find the Indies from the Crown of Castile.

In 1492, Columbus launched the first of four voyages to sail across the Atlantic and reach the Americas, arriving in the so-called "New World" in the process and unleashing an entirely new era in human history. Of course, Native Americans had lived on the North American continent for thousands of years already, after migrating there from Asia during the last glacial period.

So, Columbus was the first *European* to make it to the "New World," right? Well, that's the official narrative of events. But in recent years, new evidence has come to light. It's not just the origins of Columbus that remain clouded in mystery to this day. As we'll soon see, there may be more to Columbus than meets the eye.

****

The official reason for the voyages of Columbus was to establish a westward, seafaring route from Europe to the West Indies. Columbus was inspired by the exploits of Marco Polo and carried copies of his maps and the book *The Travels of Marco Polo* with him on his quest.

Columbus and his three ships (*Santa Maria*, *Pinta*, and *Nina*) set out from Andalusia in Spain into the Atlantic. The trio of ships first sailed to the Canary Islands, where they made repairs and stocked up on more food and water.

The ships then set sail for five weeks out into the ocean. After much trial and hardship on the open seas that tested the loyalty of the crew, they eventually caught sight of the islands that would one day be called the Bahamas. Columbus claimed that he was the first man to have caught sight of the land (thus securing a promised lifetime pension from the Spanish monarchy) and landed ashore on the island.

Columbus named the island San Salvador, which means "Holy Savior." He then called the inhabitants Los Indios, or Indians, a name which sticks to this day.

The natives (which include the Arawak, Lucayan, and Taino tribes) did not offer Columbus any kind of resistance, and as a result, Columbus did not set about constructing a defensive outpost yet.

For the next several months, Columbus explored the Caribbean, making landfall in Cuba later that year and Hispaniola after that. *Santa Maria* was forced to be abandoned when it ran aground, and Columbus used the cannons on *Nina* to open fire on the grounded ship in a show of force to the native peoples.

The only natives who offered battle to Columbus were the Ciguayo tribe, but they were quickly subdued when Columbus's men wounded two Ciguayo warriors with their weapons.

Before he left, Columbus offered to leave around 40 men in the settlement of La Navidad, which was founded in modern-day Haiti. This settlement took many natives prisoner for use as slaves to help construct the outposts and buildings.

When Columbus returned to Spain in 1493, the news that he had discovered lands to the west spread like wildfire. Columbus submitted a report to the Spanish court, which then distributed copies throughout Europe. News of Columbus's discovery spread much faster than news of da Gama's or Magellan's discoveries would in the years to come. The general consensus was that Columbus had made it to Asia.

****

Impressed by Columbus's voyage, the Castilian monarchy provided financing for a much larger expedition to return to the Americas later that year. In late September 1493, Columbus again set sail from Spain, this time with 17 ships and 15,000 men, intending to establish a permanent colony in the "New World." Farmers, soldiers, priests, carpenters, and stonemasons were among the people in Columbus's crew of the second voyage.

The second voyage was completed much faster than the first, because this time Columbus knew to set sail in a more southerly direction. Returning to the Caribbean, Columbus discovered many more islands and gave them names that many still have to this day including Saint Martin, the Virgin Islands, and Antigua.

Columbus was able to successfully navigate a return to Hispaniola, where he discovered that the La Navidad settlement was in ruins, having been overrun by the natives. In his discussions with the natives, Columbus learned that the 40 men he had left behind had become very aggressive in seeking women and gold, and when their antagonism had gone too far, they were slaughtered by native warriors.

To maintain power after learning of the massacre, Columbus reportedly became very brutal in his dealings with both the natives and the Spanish colonists. He would severely punish Spanish colonists for minor crimes, and when the death penalty was pronounced, Columbus's favored method of execution was dismemberment. Additionally, Columbus enslaved thousands of natives and subjected them to hard physical labor to help the colonists construct new settlements.

In 1495, Columbus forcefully rounded up over 15,000 Arawak men, women, and children, and shipped 500 of them back to Spain to be forced into slave labor. Around 200 of the Arawaks tragically perished during the trip.

Columbus returned to Spain in 1496, but not before the Spanish had sent more ships, supplies, and colonists to the region to reinforce the settlements that were growing there.

Columbus would remain in Europe for two years until 1498 when he set sail again with another fleet of six ships. This expedition went further south than the previous expeditions, eventually landing in what is now Venezuela. This confirmed the previous reports that there was a large continental landmass to the south of the islands that the Columbus expeditions had been visiting.

Columbus then returned to the settlements in Hispaniola only to find that the Spanish colonists were now in open revolt against his rule. Yet again, Columbus turned to sheer force to ensure his will. Using the men who had accompanied him on his ships, Columbus overcame the rebel leaders and had them either executed by hanging or sentenced to hard physical labor.

This incident taught Columbus that he would need more administrators loyal to him to help him govern the settlements. He sent two ships back to Spain requesting a Royal Commissioner who would assist him in governing the islands.

What Columbus didn't know, however, is that reports of his violent and brutal leadership style had already reached the Spanish Crown as well. Not knowing who to trust, the Crown dispatched Francisco de Bobadilla (a close friend and confidant of the Castilian Queen Isabella) to investigate.

When de Bobadilla arrived in Santo Domingo, he confirmed the reports of Columbus's brutality from the other inhabitants of the island. For example, de Bobadilla was told that Columbus would punish anyone found guilty of stealing food by having their ears and noses cut off and then subjected to hard physical labor. He also ordered the dismemberment of the bodies of any natives who revolted or fought back against them before parading their gruesome corpses in front of the other settlers.

Shocked by these reports, de Bobadilla declared himself Governor of Santo Domingo and seized Columbus's house and property on the island. He then ordered the arrest of Columbus and his brother, Diego.

Columbus denied the accusations that were leveled against him fiercely, but de Bobadilla refused to listen and had Columbus and Diego shipped back in chains to Spain. Regardless of whether the accusations against Columbus were true, it is widely believed by scholars that de Bobadilla used the accusations as an excuse to usurp Columbus and seize power of the settlements in the New World for himself.

In late 1500, Columbus arrived back in Spain as a prisoner. He was held in prison for six weeks until he was released on the orders of King Ferdinand, at which point he was summoned to the royal palace in Granada.

The monarchy had decided that de Bobadilla had taken advantage of the accusations for his own purposes and ordered him to pay restitution for the property that he had seized. They also restored wealth and freedom to Columbus and after much deliberation and debate agreed to fund a fourth voyage to the New World. Nicolas de Ovando was selected as de Bobadilla's replacement.

****

For Columbus's fourth voyage, he had at his disposal four ships and 140 men. De Bobadilla, however, had refused the royal order to stand down as Governor and denied Columbus port into Hispaniola.

Columbus would be saved by an incoming hurricane. While Columbus's four ships were able to evade the storm, de Bobadilla's 30 vessels became caught right in the middle of it. The result was an utter catastrophe. Of the ships, 20 were lost to the sea and the other 10 were severely damaged. Five hundred men were drowned in the storm, including de Bobadilla.

With de Bobadilla and most of his followers eliminated, Columbus reasserted control over the New World colonies. After resupplying his four vessels in Jamaica, he then sailed further eastward, eventually coming to the coast of Honduras. He spent two months sailing up and down the Central American coastlines, visiting what is now Nicaragua and Costa Rica in the process. Columbus attempted to find a strait that would grant access to the oceans beyond but to no avail.

Disaster struck when another storm occurred that severely damaged all four of Columbus's ships and left him and over 200 of his men stranded in Jamaica. Columbus sent a canoe of six men to Hispaniola for help, but he was denied rescue by de Ovando, who like de Bobadilla before him sought the opportunity to usurp Columbus.

Columbus and his men were nonetheless rescued by others who had heard word of his stranding. Columbus then set sail again for Spain in 1504. It would be his last time in the New World.

****

Columbus suffered from severe health issues throughout his life, which were worsened by the physical and mental toll of the four voyages. Columbus would spend the last few years of his life protesting the Spanish crown to protect the financial and political privileges of his family, and he passed away at the age of 54 in Valladolid, Spain.

Today, Columbus's name is widely known for how, in his attempt to locate a westward sea route to the Indies, he voyaged to the Americas by accident.

But was Columbus *really* the first European to locate the Americas? And did Columbus really believe that he was looking for the Indies when he sailed west? As discussed earlier, Columbus's early years are clouded in doubt. The answers to the above questions are even murkier.

An increasing amount of evidence has shown that Columbus was not the first European to visit the Americas. Far from it.

For example, there's a large amount of evidence that the Polynesians had visited the western coasts of South and Central America. It's already known that the Polynesians explored vast swaths of the Pacific using massive double canoes and colonized Fiji, Samoa, Tonga, and the Cook

Islands. Some went further south to establish settlements in New Zealand, while others continued to travel in other directions to establish settlements in the Hawaiian Islands and the Marquesas islands.

This view is supported by evidence that Polynesian tribes and South American tribes exchanged chickens and sweet potatoes with one another. It certainly explains why there were chickens in South America (when the species are native to southern Asia) and why the Polynesians got their hands on sweet potatoes, which are originally from South America.

There's also a large amount of evidence that the Vikings established settlements in what is now Canada before Columbus arrived as well. Eric the Red, for instance, gave Greenland its name and his son, Leif, started a settlement in Newfoundland where they came into armed conflict with Native American tribes.

The tales of the Vikings making landfall in the Americas were considered myths until archeological remnants of Norse settlements were discovered in Newfoundland, confirming that the old tales were true.

All the same, ancient Egyptian artifacts being discovered in the Grand Canyon of Arizona and Phoenician inscriptions and artifacts being found in what is now the southeastern United States suggest that far more ancient civilizations may have already lived in the Americas as well. Debate rages to this day about whether these findings are real or forgeries.

Of course, it's easy to assume that, while the above groups of people may have already arrived in the Americas before Columbus, these landings were still largely or entirely unknown to Europeans. But even this has been cast into doubt.

What if instead of Columbus attempting to find a seafaring route to the Indies and only accidentally stumbling across the Americas, he instead knew exactly where he was going?

****

This theory began to gain more prominence because of Columbus's association with the Knights of Christ, a remnant order of the Knights Templar. If you recall from our earlier discussion on Vasco da Gama, he was associated with this organization as well.

The Knights Templar were eliminated in 1312 in a plot conspired by the King of France, Philip, and the Catholic Pope Clement V. The Templars were accused of heresy, and many of their order were captured and killed.

It was also believed that the Templars had recovered ancient secrets and knowledge from excavations they had conducted at several sites, including in Jerusalem. From this knowledge, it was believed that they had gained knowledge of the Americas and made voyages there.

When the Templars were wiped out, the few who survived fled to two countries that offered safe refuge: Portugal and Scotland.

In Scotland, the Templar survivors were believed to have found refuge with the ruling Sinclair clan led by the Barons of Roslin. The theory is that the surviving Templars eventually founded the new order of Freemasons, who constructed the Rosslyn Chapel just outside of Edinburgh. It was also in Scotland that we have the first historical references to fraternal orders of stonemasons, suggesting that Freemasonry originated there. This would certainly help to explain the supposed Templar symbols that were engraved into the interior of the chapel.

For example, the carvings within Rosslyn Chapel depict certain things that were supposed to be unknown to Europeans at that time, such as corn maize that was native only to the Americas. This naturally poses the question: How were the men who created Rosslyn Chapel aware of corn maize? One theory that builds off of this is that the Sinclair (or St. Clair) families (and in particular Henry Sinclair in the late 1300s) conducted voyages across the North Atlantic into the Americas, building off of what the Vikings had already accomplished in the years prior.

If true, this would mean that the existence of the Americas was already known to certain Europeans who possessed access to "hidden knowledge" that was not well-known to the public. This knowledge may have been possessed by the Templars before being handed down to the Sinclair families and others who were a part of the Mason guilds.

Meanwhile, in Portugal, the Portuguese King Denis refused to prosecute members of the Templars who fled into the country. He offered them refuge and in 1319 revived their order under a new name: the Military Order of Christ.

Just like with the Templars who had fled north into Scotland, it's suggested that the Templars who fled to Portugal likewise possessed knowledge of the existence of the

Americas. After all, if ancient seafaring peoples like the Phoenicians and the Egyptians had already discovered the Americas, it's more than possible that the Templars could have uncovered the evidence of this in their excavations and search for hidden and esoteric knowledge in the Middle East and Jerusalem.

Adding to the intrigue is how Columbus married into the Military Order of Christ. Columbus's wife, Filipa Perestrelo, was the daughter of Bartolomeu Perestrelo, who was at one time the Grand Master in the Military Order of Christ.

Bartolomeu Perestrelo was a known navigator who had access to many ancient maps, charts, and logs, some of which were created many, many years ago.

How likely is it then that Columbus had access to these ancient maps from his father-in-law as well? And how likely is it that these maps could have included the Americas?

The most commonly accepted narrative for Columbus's early life is that he grew up in the Italian city of Genoa. This is significant if true because Genoa is located very close to Seborga, which was the original headquarters of the Templar order.

Now the argument that Columbus had foreknowledge of the Americas gets even more compelling. As it turns out, Columbus didn't just have connections to the Order of Christ. He also had connections to the St. Clair (Sinclair) family in Scotland as well.

After marrying Filipa Perestrelo, Columbus moved to the Madeira islands, where he met a man named John Drummond, who had also married into the Perestrelo family.

This may seem insignificant, except for the fact that Drummond was the grandson of Henry Sinclair - the same Henry Sinclair who may have voyaged to North America in the late 1300s.

What exactly Columbus and Drummond discussed is unknown to this day. It's also unknown if Columbus definitively had access to the maps of his father-in-law and if those maps contained depictions of the Americas.

But the coincidences are simply too great to ignore. It's a fact that there is an abundance of rumors and whispers that the Templars had visited the Americas (both before and after their official dissolution), and that while the early life of Columbus is shrouded in mystery, it is known that he had Templar connections.

Later in his life, Columbus began to use a very distinctive signature at the end of his letters and journal entries as well. The most prominent feature of this signature was a hooked X, which is very similar to a hooked X that the Templars were known to use as well. This further fueled the theory that Columbus was, in fact, a Templar.

Then there is the name of one of Columbus's ships. *Pinta*, one of the three vessels that Columbus used for his initial voyage, was originally named *Santa Clara* (Portuguese for St. Clair) before Columbus had it renamed *Pinta*. Did Columbus rename the ship to help hide his associations with the St. Clair family?

If Columbus indeed had access to Templar maps of North America via his connections to the Sinclair and Perestrelo families, it completely changed the narrative of his voyage to the Americas. Namely, Columbus may not have gone to the Americas to chart a course to the Indies and arrived in the Americas by accident. Instead, he may have known exactly where he was going and journeyed to the Americas intentionally to reveal it to the rest of the world.

Was there a larger plot at work, comprising the Templars and their associates, who had decided that the time had come to unveil the existence of the Americas to the world?

Or did Columbus strike out on his own and use the ancient Templar maps he may have had access to as a guide?

No one knows the answers to these questions either. But here's an idea adding another layer to the mystery: What if Columbus's voyage in 1492 to the Americas was actually not his first voyage there?

****

In 1477, Columbus arrived in Galway on the western coast of Ireland and set sail from the West. It's been commonly accepted that Columbus didn't make it far and turned back to Europe.

But in a letter to his son, Columbus wrote how, in 1477, he sailed 100 leagues westward, and discovered an island that was the same size as England. Was Columbus describing a North American landmass (like Nova Scotia or Newfoundland) to this son? Had he gotten there just like Henry Sinclair who may have gone in 1398?

What ultimately makes Columbus's story so fascinating is not just how he crossed the Atlantic to reach the Americas and how this sent shockwaves all over the world. It's the idea that Columbus, based purely on his familial connections and sheer level of coincidences in his life, may have had access to Templar maps of the Americas before he embarked on his voyage.

If Columbus indeed knew about the existence of the Americas and knew he was sailing there all along and under the guise of finding a westward route to Asia, then what was the true reason for his voyage? Was there a "hidden hand" at work here involving the Sinclair families and the remnants of the Templars that Columbus was secretly a part of? Was there a greater conspiracy at work?

Or is the commonly accepted version of Columbus's life, that he sailed to find a westward route to Asia and came to America purely by accident, would this be true after all?

There are many questions about Columbus's life and his mission but not a lot of clear answers.

This leads us into our next chapter on Amerigo Vespucci, where the gravy of this mystery continues to thicken. Columbus would not be the only European who was famous for sailing to and exploring the Americas. As it turns out, there may be more to Europeans reaching the Americas and its subsequent unveiling to the world that, if true, completely changes our understanding of human history.

WAS AMERICA
REALLY NAMED AFTER
AMERIGO VESPUCCI?

Columbus was not the only European famous for exploring the Americas. Amerigo Vespucci was an Italian explorer who made incredible discoveries in South America. The name "America" is commonly attributed to Vespucci's first name. But as it turns out, the real reason for the name "America" may have a deeper meaning than has been traditionally thought.

It is a little-known fact that Christopher Columbus was largely forgotten in his lifetime. Yes, the news of his journey to lands west of the Atlantic spread rapidly throughout Europe. But at the time, it was largely believed that Columbus had landed in Asia.

Another Italian explorer by the name of Amerigo Vespucci is the man who is credited with realizing that the Americas were not a part of Asia but rather an entirely new continent previously unknown to Europeans. It was this news that sent further shockwaves throughout the world. Further, Columbus had also largely fallen out of favor with the Spanish nobility toward the end of his life. It was also Vespucci who helped coin the term "New World" to describe these new lands.

But with Amerigo Vespucci, we arrive at another mystery. The name "America" is usually thought to have been a reference to Vespucci. However recent evidence has emerged that there may be another reason separate from Vespucci, which we'll discuss later in this chapter.

This isn't to say that Vespucci should be overlooked. Even though he was very famous in his day, in the hundreds of years since, the name Vespucci largely fell by the wayside as Columbus gained more prominence. But Vespucci was undeniably one of the most accomplished figures of the Age of Discovery.

As with Columbus, there are many questions and many possible answers to each one.

****

Amerigo Vespucci was born on March 9 1451 in Florence. At the time, Florence was one of the wealthiest Italian city-states and was both a cultural and economic hub in Europe. Many of the artists of the Renaissance period, for instance, would flourish in Florence.

The Vespucci family was politically well-connected, with Amerigo's grandfather (who also bore the same name) serving for 36 years as the chancellor of Florence. The Vespucci family was also well-connected to the Medici family, who were essentially the de facto rulers of Florence for more than three centuries.

So, from a young age, Vespucci would be an established figure in Florentine politics. But on top of that, he also held an intense interest in maps and books, spending long hours at local museums and libraries studying maps and reading. The explorer that Vespucci studied most was Marco Polo, and he dreamed of traveling to unexplored lands just as Polo had done centuries before him. Vespucci was also educated by his uncle, who worked as a banker for the Medici family.

Vespucci's uncle often sailed the Mediterranean between Italy and Spain due to the nature of his work for the Médicis. Young Amerigo became fascinated watching the great explorer ships sailing in and out of the harbor and took a special interest in observing how the ships were outfitted, stocked, and repaired.

He also familiarized himself with the kinds of spices and goods that came into the harbor as well. Silk and tea were coming in from China, spices were coming in from India and Indonesia, and coffee and salt were coming in from Africa. Vespucci engaged in conversations with the sailors and explorers, learning even more about these faraway lands than he had already read about in books.

Vespucci was the kind of man who was born into the right century. He had an intense interest in exploration and navigation from the time he was young, and he was born right in the middle of the Age of Exploration and trade. Back then, Europeans were searching for reliable seafaring routes from Europe to India and Asia. Muslims controlled most of the land-based trade leading into China and India, and they inflicted high prices upon the Christians of Europe to take part in this trade.

By looking to the oceans, the Europeans were able to look for a cheaper route to engage in trade with those in Asia without interference from the Muslims. But the oceans were no more forgiving than land journeys, and expeditions from Europe to faraway lands such as Asia or Africa commonly took several years to accomplish.

The Vespucci family became active in the exploration and trading industry early on. They helped to provision and outfit ships for voyages from Europe to the Indies and beyond. In fact, the Vespucci family business helped to outfit one of the voyages Columbus took west to what was believed to be the Indies (when in reality, it was North America).

In 1496, Vespucci was even able to meet Columbus and acquire much valuable advice on seafaring and exploring. The meeting with Columbus was an instrumental moment in Vespucci's life because it reactivated the interest in navigation and exploration that he had in his youth.

Vespucci was driven by a deep internal desire to travel the world and explore areas that were previously unknown to human eyes, at least to those who lived in Europe. As interest in geography, astronomy, cartography, and new civilizations was growing in general, Vespucci felt even more compelled to become a major player in the exploration age.

Vespucci gradually became discontented with his career in the family business of outfitting ships for travel and exploration. Rather than merely helping to outfit a ship for exploration, Vespucci wanted to get in on the action himself!

Even though Vespucci was living a comfortable life in Seville and was happily married to a Spanish woman, Vespucci's thirst for adventure would prove to be too great.

****

Attempting to piece together the story of Vespucci's voyages is difficult because of how little we know. Almost all of the evidence for Vespucci's voyages comes from letters that were either written by him or were believed to be written by him. Since these letters are sometimes piecemeal and other times have large gaps in between them, it's hard to figure out exactly how many voyages Vespucci undertook, the routes that were taken for each voyage, and what exactly was accomplished or explored in each voyage.

What we know about Vespucci is almost the direct opposite of what we know about Columbus and da Gama. In the case of Columbus and da Gama, very little is known about their earlier lives, and much is known about their later lives and voyages. In the case of Vespucci, much more is known about his earlier life and activities than after he set sail.

What is commonly accepted by most historians, however, is that Vespucci took part in at least two voyages from Europe to the New World. While he has been alleged to have participated in more voyages (most likely two more to a total of four), the evidence for these further voyages is inconsistent at best.

The information we have for Vespucci's alleged first voyage largely comes from a letter that was written to Piero Soderini, a statesman of Florentine, in 1504. The letter explains how Vespucci departed from Spain for the newly discovered lands to the West in May 1497, and how the voyage returned around a year and a half later.

If the information in the letter is true, Vespucci traveled from Spain to Honduras, and then onward across the Caribbean to Mexico. The problem with this letter is the inaccuracy of the information, particularly with the directions and descriptions that Vespucci provided in them. Some argue this inaccurate information was because of a forgery, while others argue that Vespucci simply miscalculated.

Vespucci's second voyage is more rounded in specific facts and is commonly accepted by historians as having actually happened. This voyage took place in 1499 and was licensed by Spain. Vespucci did not lead this voyage but rather worked for Alonso de Ojeda and Juan de la Cosa, the commander and chief navigator, respectively.

The purpose of this voyage was simple: to explore more land in the area where Columbus had done business, and if possible, to return with rich minerals and spices for trading. Vespucci's family business would have financed two of the four ships in this expedition, but the exact role that Vespucci played in it is not overwhelmingly clear. It's most likely that Vespucci served in a leadership role but was subservient to de Ojeda and de la Cosa.

Regardless, the four ships departed Spain in May 1499. Customary of most voyages to the New World at that time, the ships first stopped in the Canary Islands for repairs and to restock their supplies before continuing onward to the New World.

The ships finally came to South America, landing in what is now French Guiana on the northeastern South American coast. After arriving in South America, the fleet split. Ojeda led two ships north along the coastline of what is now Venezuela. Meanwhile, the other two ships moved southward. Vespucci would have been aboard the southbound ships.

At the time, Vespucci also believed that they were in Asia, and he thought that the ships were along the eastern coastline of the Asian continent. Vespucci and his men thought that by continuing to move down the South American coastline, they would eventually round the continent and come out into the Indian Ocean.

The southward sailing, however, did not go well. The current moving in the opposite direction could not be overcome by the two ships, so they were forced to turn around and explore northward instead. The ships continued working their way up the South American coast, eventually coming to the coast of what is now Venezuela before rejoining Ojeda and then moving north for Hispaniola, where the Spanish had a colony which we discussed in the chapter on Columbus.

After resting and restocking supplies in Hispaniola, the fleet traveled to the Bahamas, where they captured more than 200 slaves to be sold in Spain. The fleet then resailed across the Atlantic back to Spain.

****

Vespucci's third alleged voyage would have occurred in 1501. King Manuel I of Portugal elected to fund an expedition to investigate a landmass that had been discovered to the west. This landmass (which would eventually be realized to be South America) was positioned to the south of the colonies in the Caribbean.

The purpose of this voyage would be to determine which lands in this new landmass could be claimed by Portugal under the Treaty of Tordesillas, which was designed to divide new lands between Spain and Portugal.

Vespucci commanded this expedition, his reputation as a skilled navigator and natural leader having been strengthened following his second voyage. The fleet departed Lisbon in May 1501 for Cape Verde off the western coast of Africa. After resupplying at Cape Verde, the fleet set sail across the Atlantic.

The expedition eventually landed along the coastline of what is now Brazil. Moving onto land, the crew immediately encountered hostile and cannibalistic natives, who captured and later killed and ate one of the crew members. The fleet then sailed further south to find native tribes who would be friendlier, which they eventually did in the bay of what is now Rio de Janeiro, which was formally established on January 1, 1502.

Vespucci's crew remained in Rio de Janeiro for a month, where they enjoyed interacting and trading with the natives. The fleet then left Rio and set sail back for home.

Vespucci is also believed by some historians to have taken part in a fourth voyage to explore what is now Brazil, but only one letter from Vespucci is used as evidence for this voyage, and some historians dispute Vespucci's authorship of this letter as well.

****

Even though we know very little about the details of Vespucci's voyages (and alleged voyages), what is known is that when he returned home to Seville by 1505, he had developed a solid reputation as a navigator and an explorer. His reputation was so strong that King Ferdinand of Spain did not hold a grudge or bear ill will against Vespucci for his service to his chief competitor, King Manuel I of Portugal.

Vespucci would continue to remain loyal to the Spanish crown until he passed away in 1512. For the remainder of his life, he continued to work by helping outfit ships sailing for the Indies. Vespucci also helped train new navigators and ship crewmen to ensure they were properly trained before embarking on long voyages.

Vespucci's exploits became even more famous as a result of the letters that were circulated throughout Europe and helped spread his name further. Again, some of these letters are in dispute with regard to their accuracy and whether or not Vespucci actually authored all of them.

But without the existence of these letters, Vespucci possibly would have been completely forgotten by the history books. One letter in particular established Vespucci as the discoverer of the so-called "New World," which was now so-named because it was realized that the Americas were a completely separate continent from Asia. This letter became known as "the Soderini letter," which was re-translated into several other languages, including French. Scholars at a French university in Lorraine read the Soderini leather and publicly announced that the letter concerned a voyage to an entirely new continent rather than Asia.

Since Vespucci was supposedly the author of the letter and the leader of the voyage, the credit for the discovery of these new lands was given to him. The news soon spread over the world.

Two of the men who read the Soderini letter and made this announcement that the lands discovered were new were Martin Waldseemuller and Matthias Ringmann. When they created a world map in their *Introduction to Cosmography* book, they argued that the "New World" should be named after Vespucci. They proposed *America* since America was the feminine version of *Amerigo,* Vespucci's first name. The men wanted to give a female name to America because feminine names had also been provided to Europe and Asia.

Waldseemuller and Ringmann's world map spread quickly throughout Europe. A thousand copies were created, and Amerigo Vespucci's name was attached to these maps along with his portrait. This was the very first time *America* was used to describe the New World.

The maps created by Waldseemuller and Ringmann continued to be produced across multiple editions for several years and were widely utilized in universities and by other famous mapmakers. The name "America" spread far and wide.

****

Except..., was America *really* named after Amerigo Vespucci?

This has been taken as a commonly accepted fact for years, but as is the case with Columbus, new research and information have cast doubt on what we know about Vespucci and the role he played in discovering the Americas.

For one thing, Amerigo was not even Vespucci's real first name. His real first name was Alberigo. If Vespucci ever changed his name to Amerigo, it would have happened after he sailed back to Europe from the Americas. This begs the question: Why would he change his name?

As we mentioned previously in this book, a variety of ancient artifacts were discovered in Europe as well, which further casts doubt on the commonly accepted narrative that Columbus was the first European to discover the Americas. In fact, it's now believed that the Vikings landed in what is now Canada long before Columbus did. The ancient Egyptian artifacts found in the Grand Canyon in Arizona and Phoenician artifacts found along the eastern North American coastline further make us wonder about other ancient peoples in the Americas.

This then makes us wonder if Europeans too, and specifically members of European secret societies such as the St. Clair family, had already landed in the Americas as well.

So why would Vespucci change his first name from Alberigo to Amerigo after he returned home from his voyages?

What if the Americas were not really named after Vespucci at all? What if, instead, Vespucci based his name change after America, and then Waldseemuller and Ringmann named the lands on their maps after Vespucci?

There is increasingly compelling evidence to support this theory, that Amerigo actually came from America, and not the other way around like we are commonly taught.

The initial primary supporter of this theory was a French geologist in the 1800s named Jules Marcou. Marcou was studying America and its history when he first posited the theory that Vespucci had changed his name to reflect the New World and not the other way around.

According to Marcou's research, Vespucci signed his name as Alberigo and not Amerigo in his early letters. Also, according to Marcou, the civilizations living in the Americas such as the Mayans called their land *Amerrique*, which means "Land of the Wind", "Land of the Air" or

"Land of the Spirit" (depending on the translation and interpretation).

What was this air or spirit that the Mayans and other civilizations worshiped and followed? According to the *Popol Vuh*, which is the Mayan narrative of how the Earth was created, the creator was a feathered serpent named Q'uq'umatz. This god was referred to by the Aztecs in what is now Mexico as "Quetzalcoatl" or as "Amaru" by the Incas in what is now Peru.

Thus, another translation of the name *Amerrique* would be *Amaruca*, which simply means "Land of the Plumed Serpent" according to most translations and interpretations.

If this is the case, then it could be surmised that Vespucci learned the names *Amerrique* or *Ameruca* and then changed his name to Amerigo after his voyages to reflect the new lands that he had explored.

America was not really named after Vespucci. Rather, Vespucci was named after America.

****

The popular narrative for the founding of America goes something like this: America was first reached from Europe by Christopher Columbus, named after Amerigo Vespucci, and over the next several centuries, waves of immigrants from Europe sailed across the Atlantic for a new life in the New World.

Eventually, colonies were established all across North and South America under the leadership of established European countries, most notably Great Britain, France, Spain, and Portugal. Then when the 13 American colonies rebelled and succeeded in their rebellion against Britain, they founded the United States.

But what if there's more to the story? What if there were, in fact, multiple pre-Columbian European voyages to the New World and that the idea of reaching a new country in the New World was planned and hundreds of years in the making?

There is strong evidence that the Phoenicians and Egyptians landed in America in ancient times based on artifacts that have been left behind and that the Sinclair families landed in what is now Newfoundland and New England based on their writings.

According to Manly P. Hall, a Canadian historian and Freemason, "The explorers who opened the New World operated from a master plan and were agents of re-discovery rather than discoverers. Very little is known about the origin, lives, characters, and policies of these intrepid adventurers. Although they lived in a century amply provided with historians and biographers, these saw fit either to remain silent or to invent plausible accounts without substance."

In other words, according to Hall, there was already vast knowledge of the Americas among secret societies. The explorers who landed in them like Vespucci and Columbus were in fact not the first Europeans to do so but rather operating with secret societies to unveil the existence of these lands to the rest of the known world. That's fascinating to think about because it completely changes the way that we view history.

According to the writings, Francis Bacon, an English statesman who served under King James I and helped to lead the advancement of the scientific method, many ancient societies such as the Rosicrucians were seeking to create a new country, a "New Atlantis" in the Americas that would help lead the world into a new state of enlightenment.

All the same, Bacon referred to the lands of the New World as *Amaruca* as well, adding credence to the idea that the

87

ancient societies knew these lands long before Columbus arrived and that they were not named after Vespucci after all. This then supports the theory that the establishment of the United States was perhaps planned by secret societies long in advance.

Vespucci may have explored much of the coastlines of South America and the Caribbean. And when he arrived in the Americas, he had much reverence for these lands, for the lands of Amaruca. So much so, that perhaps he changed his first name to reflect the new lands he had visited. It was not the Americas that bore the name of Amerigo Vespucci, but rather Vespucci who bore the name of America.

Not long after Vespucci was exploring the Caribbean and the coastlines of South America, another famous European explorer would sail to the opposite side of South America and explore the lands of what is now Peru. This man's name was Francisco Pizarro, and he was a man of conquest.

FRANCISCO PIZARRO'S CONQUEST OF PERU

Spanish conquistador Francisco Pizarro grew up impoverished but was determined to find his fortune in the so-called New World. Pizarro crossed the Panamanian Isthmus and conquered the Incas in what is today Peru, founding the modern-day city of Lima. But Pizarro's thirst for conquest and fame would prove to be his ultimate undoing.

Francisco Pizarro's full name was Francisco Pizarro Gonzalez. He would become one of the most famous Spanish conquistadors of all time.

Unlike other famous explorers we have discussed thus far like Marco Polo, Columbus, Magellan, or Vespucci, Pizarro was not born into a politically privileged family, working with the monarchies of the day, or actively involved in the exploration or trading industry. But that didn't deter Pizarro.

Pizarro was born in a poor family in Trujillo, Spain as the illegitimate son of an infantry Colonel named Gonzalez Pizarro. Pizarro grew up illiterate and uneducated. However, perhaps by sheer coincidence, Pizzaro was a second cousin once removed of Hernan Cortes, another famous conquistador who would become known for conquering the Aztec Empire in what is now Mexico.

From his youth, Pizarro had an avid interest in exploration and adventure. He joined a ship commanded by Alonso de Ojeda that was sailing on an expedition from Spain to the New World, and specifically now what is the coast of Colombia. While little is known about this stage of Pizarro's life, we do know that Ojeda attempted to establish a colony in what is now the Gulf of Uraba in Colombia. When this colony failed, Pizarro established leadership over the survivors and abandoned the area with them.

Pizarro then sailed to Cartagena, joining a fleet commanded by Vasco Nunez de Balboa and crossing the Isthmus of Panama into the Pacific Ocean. The finding of the Isthmus of Panama was significant because it provided a much faster route to enter the Pacific than sailing all the way around the southern tip of South America.

A year later, Pizarro began working closely with Balboa's successor, Pedro Arias Davila. Davila was a very cruel man. He assigned Pizarro to oversee the native slave labor system. Davila later had Balboa beheaded, believing he wasn't sufficiently loyal. For the part that Pizarro played in the capture and delivery of Balboa to his trial, Davila rewarded him by naming him Mayor of Alcalde and as magistrate of Panama City, which had recently been established.

Pizarro later took part in the explorations of the west coast of South America. There was intense interest in western South America because of reports of a gold-rich area on a river called Piru, which was later renamed "Peru."

A conquistador by the name of Pascual de Andagoya had already undertaken explorations of western South America, establishing contact with several native tribes there. Andagoya heard much from the natives about the gold-rich lands, but he was forced to return to Panama when he became ill during the trip.

Pizarro heard these stories from Andagoya about rich stocks of gold, and news had also come of Hernan Cortes's successful conquest of the Aztecs in what is now Mexico.

Pizarro was eager to replicate the success of Cortes further south and discover gold in the process.

****

Pizarro's first expedition down the western coastline of South America took place in late 1524. Departing from Panama, the voyage set sail with 80 men and four horses and was approved by the Panamanian Governor Pedro Davila. The expedition was rapidly cut short as a lack of food and repeated encounters with hostile natives forced the expedition to turn around.

Pizarro's second expedition took place in early 1526 and again was approved by the Panamanian governor. Pizarro set sail from Panama, this time with two ships holding several horses and over 160 men. The two ships made it down to the San Juan River in modern-day Colombia and then split up. Pizarro stayed to explore the area, while one of his co-commanders, Almagro, led a ship back to Panama to secure reinforcements.

The other co-commander, Bartolome Ruiz, led another ship to continue sailing south. Ruiz encountered natives from Peru, who had textiles and emeralds, silver, and gold with them, confirming Pizarro's belief that there was gold to be found in Peru.

When Ruiz returned to Pizarro, he and his men were exhausted from exploring the area. Almagro then returned as well with more supplies and 80 more men who had arrived in Panama from Spain. Ruiz's news that he had discovered natives with gold and precious metals was very welcome news for Pizarro.

The reunited expedition continued to work their way south down the Spanish coastline, encountering many hostile native forces along the way. Some of these native peoples were serving the larger Incan Empire.

Almagro returned to Panama again for more reinforcements, while Pizarro stayed at the Isla de Gallo. When Almagro got back to Panama, however, the new governor Pedro de los Rios had lost faith in Pizarro. He rejected Almagro's request for more men and resources and ordered two ships led by Juan Tafur to be dispatched to bring Pizarro back to Panama.

Tafur sailed south, eventually reaching the Isla de Gallo where Pizarro was.

Famously, when Pizarro rejected Tafur's demands to return north, Pizarro drew a line in the sand and declared, "There lies Peru with its riches. Here, Panama and its poverty. Choose, each man, what best becomes a brave Castilian. For my part, I go to the south."

Only 13 men chose to follow Pizarro, and these men became known as the *Los Trece de la Fama,* meaning "the Famous Thirteen." The other men joined with Tafur.

Pizarro and his 13 men constructed a rather crude boat and journeyed north to the La Isla Gorgona. They stayed there for 13 months until they were rejoined by Almagro in a ship. Almagro had finally convinced Governor de los Rios to commission another ship to go south and bring Pizarro back within six months. Almagro took the ship and left Panama for La Isla Gorgona.

There, Pizarro and his men elected to continue sailing south, eventually coming to the Tumbes Region of Peru in the Spring of 1528. For the first time in a long while, Pizarro and his men were actually greeted warmly by the native tribes, the Tumpis. Some of Pizarro's men had conducted reconnaissance of the Tumpis' villages and returned to Pizarro with news of silver and gold on the residences of the chiefs.

Coming ashore, Pizarro was greeted warmly by the Tumpis, who also reported to him the existence of a wealthy and powerful king who ruled over all the people in the area.

Pizarro was eager to meet this king, but he also knew that he and his few men would be heavily outnumbered in the event of a violent confrontation. He decided it would be wiser to sail back north for Panama, secure new supplies and reinforcements, and then return south. Pizarro left two of his men to learn the local language and customs of the Tumpis, and in exchange, two Tumpis boys joined him on the ship to travel back to Panama and learn Spanish.

****

When Pizarro returned to Panama, Governor de los Rios refused to commission another voyage to travel to Peru. Pizarro was thus forced to go to Spain to appeal to the monarchy in person. He brought with him the natives, llamas, and samples of silver and gold to show to King Charles I and Queen Isabelle.

Unlike de los Rios, Charles I and Isabelle were both hugely impressed by Pizarro's tales of riches in Peru. The two commissioned Pizarro to conquer Peru for Spain, and Pizarro was named as the governor of Peru. This was all officially ratified by Queen Isabella in the *Capitulacion de Toledo* in 1529.

Pizarro also returned to Trujillo, where he was from, and met with his brother and two half-brothers (Hernando, Juan, and Gonzalo) and several other close friends and cousins. He informed them of the riches that he had discovered in Peru and requested that they join him on his great expedition.

When the expedition left for Peru the next year, there were nearly 30 horses and 180 men aboard two ships. This would be Pizarro's third and final expedition.

****

Pizarro returned to South America in 1531. He reunited with Almagro, who had gathered more recruits from Panama. The expedition landed in the Coaque region of Ecuador, where they discovered and took possession of large quantities of emeralds, gold, and silver.

The expedition was then reinforced by the arrival of Hernando de Soto, who had 100 men-at-arms with him.

The ships sailed south to the Tumbes region, but to their dismay, the party found the local villages that had treated them with hospitality before had been ransacked and destroyed. Many of the native Tumbis had been killed by other tribes.

Pizarro resolved to lead a Spanish expedition deep into the interior, and in May 1532, he established the first Spanish settlement in Peru called "San Miguel de Piura." Pizarro left 50 men at this establishment before leading 200 into the South American interior.

De Soto moved on ahead, and a week later he returned with an Incan envoy with an invitation to come see the king. The Incas were the largest native empire in South America, with their capital based out of Cusco.

At this time, the Incas had been waging a brutal civil war with one another. Known as the War of the Two Brothers, it was fought between half-brothers Atahualpa and Huascar for the throne of the Incan empire following the death of their father. Atahualpa had emerged victorious from the conflict by the time Pizarro and his men arrived.

The Incan civil war that had ravaged South America was brutal and bloody. It had involved hundreds of thousands of soldiers on both sides with thousands killed and several Incan towns devastated. As a result, the Incan Empire was left severely weakened by the time Pizarro was on the scene.

Atahualpa had been resting in the Sierra mountains of northern Peru after defeating his brother Huascar. He was enjoying himself in the hot Inca Baths when Pizarro and his small force arrived. Pizarro had at his disposal over 100 infantry soldiers, nearly 70 cavalrymen, two cannons, and three arquebus rifles.

Pizarro dispatched his brother Hernando and de Soto to meet with Atahualpa, who agreed to meet with the men as well. A friar who was a part of Pizarro's force, Vincente de Valverde, explained the Christian faith and the need of the Incan King to pay tribute to Spanish Emperor Charles V, to which Atahualpa refused.

Atahualpa could have easily massacred the Spanish right then and there. Pizarro had less than 200 men, while Atahualpa had over 50,000 men with several thousand more scattered throughout the empire. But even though Atahualpa refused to grant tribute to Spain, he also did nothing to attack the Spanish, yet.

Pizarro, meanwhile, was in a tight position. He knew that his small force had no hope of defeating the Incas in battle, but to retreat would also be a display of weakness to the Incas. Pizarro realized that their only hope for success was to take possession of Incan stone fortresses, from which they could hold off an Incan attack.

Pizarro was also inspired by the success of Hernan Cortes in conquering the Aztecs of Mexico. Cortes had found himself in a very similar position to Pizarro. To ensure success, Cortes launched a daring plan to capture the Aztec King from within his own army and use him as leverage. Pizarro planned to do the same thing with Atahualpa and explained his strategy to his officers.

Pizarro invited Atahualpa to meet with him in the city of Cajamarca. Atahualpa, in a display of force, arrived amongst a huge procession of men and positioned tens of thousands of warriors outside of the city. Due to the sheer number of armed warriors Atahualpa had at his disposal, he had no fear of a possible attack or act of violence from the Spanish. This was exactly the mentality of which Pizarro sought to take advantage.

Pizarro concealed many of his men and cannons in the buildings surrounding the plaza in the center of the town.

Atahualpa entered the town square with several of his men, at which point the Spanish unleashed cannon fire and gunfire into the mass of Incans, killing or wounding several.

Pizarro's men then rushed forward and charged with bladed weapons, striking down many Incan warriors who were caught completely off guard by the attack. More Spanish cavalry on horses appeared from behind the houses and added to the confusion while Spanish infantrymen provided covering fire from above.

The small and yet fierce Spanish force closed in on Atahualpa. The men protecting Atahualpa were so shocked by the attack that they offered little resistance, and the Spanish severed their hands and arms with swords. Pizarro ordered his men to kill all of Atahualpa's bodyguards and attendants but to spare the King's life. When one of his men tried to attack Atahualpa anyway, Pizarro positioned his body in between the King and the blade, sustaining a grievous wound as a result.

Meanwhile, Atahualpa's several-thousand-man army outside the walls of the city was completely routed. The loss of their King and all of the military commanders completely demoralized them and caused many of them to drop their weapons and run away, despite being veterans of the Incan Civil War.

Just like that, Atahualpa had been captured, thousands of Incas had been killed or wounded, and not one Spanish soldier had lost their life. Almagro arrived later with reinforcements of 150 fifty men and 50 horses, strengthening the Spanish position further.

Pizarro later had Atahualpa executed publicly via garrote, which would later be condemned by King Charles of Spain, who respected Atahualpa as a fellow monarch. Several of Pizarro's men were opposed to the execution as well, but it was believed that only the death of the Incan King would convince the rest of the Incan empire to submit to the Spanish.

Pizarro strengthened his army to 500 men and then advanced on Cuzco (a.k.a. Cusco), the Incan capital, and conquered it. Pizarro was highly impressed by the architecture and complexity of Cuzco, later writing that it was the greatest and finest city that he had ever seen in his life, even greater than the big cities in which he had grown up in Spain.

Naturally, Pizarro elected also to make Cuzco the capital of the Spanish colony in Peru. However, it was deemed to be too high in the mountains, so it was determined a new capital in the lowlands and closer to the sea would be needed for the sake of convenience. Pizarro founded the city of Lima along the coastline of Peru so it would be accessible to Spanish ships. Pizarro would later write how founding Lima was one of his greatest lifetime accomplishments.

For the next several years, warfare ravaged Peru between the Incas loyal to the original empire on one side and the Spanish and the Incas allied to them on the other. The Incas managed to win a few battles and kill several Spanish soldiers, but the technological advantage of the Spanish when it came to weapons helped make them victorious. The Spanish were also able to withstand numerous Incan assaults on Cuzco thanks to its fortified walls and their use of rifles.

As more Spanish soldiers arrived, the balance of power shifted in their favor. Incan resistance gradually weakened as they came to accept their new Spanish conquerors who could not be defeated in battle. Within a few years, the Incas were completely at the mercy of the Spanish, who were shipping in more colonists and supplies regularly to strengthen their position.

But after the Spanish secured their victory over the Incas, another war broke out, and this time it was a civil war between the Spanish. This war would soon lead to the death of Pizarro.

****

Almagro and the Pizarro brothers were in a dispute about who would rule the newly established Spanish colony in Peru. Both, for instance, laid claim to Cuzco.

In the ensuing war, the Pizarro brothers emerged victorious and had Almagro captured and executed. Several Spaniards, however, remained loyal to Almagro's cause and resolved to kill Pizarro as revenge.

In June 1541, 20 heavily armed men stormed the palace where Pizarro was staying and killed him with their weapons. Pizarro was in the process of struggling to affix his armor when he was attacked. Despite managing to cut down three of his assailants with his sword, he was overwhelmed and slashed across the throat with a bladed weapon before falling to the floor. He was then stabbed numerous times all over his body by his assailants.

Pizarro was 63 years old when he died.

That may have been the end of Francisco Pizarro, but it was hardly the end of the Spanish in Peru. Pizarro had succeeded in his mission to conquer Peru for Spain, and the Incan Empire had completely collapsed as a result. He also initiated the introduction of Christianity into Peru and ordered the polytheistic sun-worshipping religion of the Incas to be disbanded and replaced. The Spanish continued to rule Peru up until the 1820s, and people there continue to speak Spanish as their native language to this day.

Pizarro's conquest of Peru is significant because he managed to completely subdue an entire empire with only a few hundred men. But ultimately, Pizarro's thirst for conquest proved to be his ultimate undoing.

As the Europeans started colonizing South America, it was only a matter of time before they would explore further out into the Pacific and beyond.

JAMES COOK
LANDS IN HAWAII

In the late 1700s, British maritime cartographer James Cook circumnavigated Antarctica, charted Australia and New Zealand and discovered numerous islands throughout the Pacific. It was when he landed in the Hawaiian Islands that he met his gruesome end.

James Cook was one of the most famous British cartographers and explorers the world has ever known. It was because of Cook that the world was provided with the geography of Newfoundland, Antarctica, New Zealand, Australia, and many islands throughout the Pacific Ocean, including Hawaii.

Cook arrived on the scene hundreds of years after the likes of Magellan or Columbus, and yet his contributions to world exploration are no less significant. Cook built very effectively upon the work of the explorers and adventurous who came before him to chart his own course around the world.

Cook was born on November 7, 1728, in Yorkshire. He was named after his father and went to work for him on a farm. Cook was also educated in his youth in astronomy, charting, and mathematics.

By Cook's time, colonies had been established by several European countries up and down the Americas. However, massive portions of North America remained unexplored, as did vast swaths of the Pacific Ocean.

When he was 16 years old, Cook went to work for a haberdasher who operated a shop right alongside the ocean. Cook would have seen ships sailing by daily while working in the shop, and it's here that he may have begun to develop a love for the sea.

Eager to go to work on a ship, Cook was hired as a merchant navy apprentice in a fleet of vessels that were transporting coal along the English coast. Cook spent three years in this position, and he continued to receive education in navigation, mathematics, and mapmaking, all of which would prove to be essential skills later in his life.

Cook then went to work as a merchant naval sailor on British trading ships operating outside of the Baltic Sea. He moved his way up the ranks, and within a year he was promoted to command the brig *Friendship*. A month later, Cook volunteered to serve in the British Royal Navy. Britain was eager to bring new hands into the British fleet as they were mobilizing for battle in the upcoming Seven Years' War that was about to erupt across Europe.

Cook was posted to serve aboard *HMS Eagle*, which engaged French vessels in battle, capturing at least one French warship and sinking another. These experiences provided Cook with combat experience at sea.

Cook was later transferred to serve aboard *HMS Pembroke*, which was dispatched to fight the French in North America. He served in an amphibious assault at the Battle of Louisbourg and in the siege of Quebec City in what is now Canada. During his service in these campaigns, Cook was noted for his skills as a surveyor, cartographer, and mapmaker. As a result, his superiors assigned him to map the entrance to the Saint Lawrence River. Cook's mapmaking skills proved invaluable to later British success in the war.

Later transferring to *HMS Grenville*, Cook was assigned to survey and map Newfoundland. Cook's maps became the first accurate and large-scale maps of the island, and they were submitted to the Royal Society, Great Britain's national academy of sciences. Cook was a master at using triangulation (or the practice of determining a point's location by forming triangles to that point) to develop precise land outlines.

The Royal Society subsequently took an interest in Cook due to his surveying and mapmaking skills. Copies of Cook's Newfoundland maps would be used by those sailing along Newfoundland's coast for the next two centuries.

Cook's career was just getting started. He would write in his diary that he intended to go "farther than any man has been before me, but as far as I think it is possible for a man to go."

****

At the age of 39, Cook departed on his first voyage in August 1768. The British Admiralty commissioned him to take command of the *HMS Endeavour* for a scientific voyage into the Pacific. Cook was selected for the mission because of his experience, the reputation he had built by mapping Newfoundland, and his participation in the campaigns in North America. Cook was promoted to lieutenant so he could legally command the voyage.

The purpose of this new voyage was simple: to observe and record the transit of Venus across the Sun. This would then help to calculate the distance between the Earth and the Sun. The transit of Venus is when the planet Venus is seen as a silhouette against the face of the Sun.

After departing from Great Britain, Cook and his crew sailed around the Cape Horn at the bottom of South America before continuing out into the Pacific. In April of the following year, *Endeavour* landed at the island of Tahiti and Cook's crew made and recorded observations of the transit.

After the observations were complete, Cook opened up his new orders, which were sealed and were not to be opened until the observations were complete. The second part of the orders was revealed: Sail around the southern Pacific in search of the continent that was then known as *Terra Australis*.

Contrary to what the name might suggest, Terra Australis was not an old name for Australia, which was already known to people back then. Rather, Terra Australis was the name given to a supposed seventh continent that was not confirmed to have existed back then - the continent of Antarctica.

To begin his search, Cook had the Endeavour sail south to New Zealand, and he mapped the entire coastline. He also interacted directly with several Māori tribes, utilizing the services of a Tahitian priest named Tupaia who had joined the expedition. Some of these interactions were peaceful and hospitable, while others were violent. At least eight Māori were recorded as being killed by Cook's men when the encounters turned aggressive.

After mapping New Zealand, Cook sailed the *Endeavour* west to reach the coastline of Australia. Cook encountered Aboriginal Australians and continued sailing along the Australian coastline, making detailed maps all along the way. The exhibition eventually stopped at what is now called Botany Bay, where the crew disembarked from the *Endeavour* and spent a full week on land gathering resources and collecting botanical specimens.

The *Endeavour* then resumed traveling around the Australian coastline but was nearly destroyed when it ran afoul of the Great Barrier Reef. The ship nearly sank! Cook retreated into a river along the Australian coastline and the party spent seven weeks repairing the ship using natural resources at their disposal. Thankfully, the crew were able to fix the ship and sail it back to England in July 1771. The entire voyage had taken nearly three years to complete.

Cook was warmly received upon his return, with his findings welcomed by the scientific community.

****

Due to the success of his mission, Cook was promoted to the rank of commander. It would be less than a year before he would be commissioned to lead a second expedition funded by the Royal Society.

While Cook had succeeded in his mission of observing the transit of Venus and drawing more detailed maps of Australia and New Zealand, he had failed to locate the fabled *Terra Australis*. However, his first mission showed that the lost continent was not connected to New Zealand or Australia, suggesting that the continent was located even further south. The Royal Society believed firmly that a huge southern continent existed.

For the new voyage, Cook was provided command of the *HMS Resolution*, while his second-in-command Tobias Furneaux commanded a second ship called the *HMS Adventure*.

The second voyage was even more wide-ranging than the first. Cook circumnavigated the entire world at a southern latitude, and he and his crew became the first Europeans to cross the Antarctic Circle and discover the fabled *Terra Australis*, which was really just Antarctica.

The fog surrounding the Antarctic was very thick, and *Resolution* and *Adventure* became separated. Unable to locate Cook, Furneaux decided to disengage the *Adventure* from exploring Antarctica and took the vessel northeast to New Zealand. After making landfall, Furneaux's men were attacked by Māori and forced to retreat to the ship. Furneaux decided to abandon the voyage and sailed back to Britain.

Meanwhile, Cook continued to explore the Antarctic coastline, which was covered in ice. Cook was searching for the actual Antarctic landmass, but unable to locate it and running low on supplies, he opted to return to Tahiti to resupply the ship. Cook then explored much of the South Pacific, mapping Easter Island, Norfolk Island, New Caledonia, Vanuatu, and the Sandwich Islands (now called Hawaii).

Cook finally rounded the southern tip of South America again, sailed east to the African coastline, and then followed the coastline back up to Great Britain by 1775. Like the first voyage, Cook's second voyage took around three years.

Cook was again warmly received and again promoted, this time to post-captain. He was also made a Fellow of the Royal Society. The maps that he made from his second voyage were still in use well into the 1900s - that's how accurate they were.

****

As with the first voyage, Cook only took roughly a year's respite before embarking on his third voyage. For this third voyage - which ultimately turned out to be his last - Cook was again provided command of the *HMS Resolution*. His second-in-command, Charles Clerke, was given command of a second ship called the *HMS Discovery*.

The purpose of the third voyage was to locate a Northwest Passage around the North American continent. Cook disembarked from England in 1776, crossed the Atlantic, sailed around the southern tip of South America, and then sailed across the Pacific to Tahiti to resupply.

After doing so, Cook's two ships traveled north in search of the Northwest Passage, eventually coming to the coastline of California and Oregon. The ships continued to sail northward along the North American coastline of what is now Washington state and Canada.

The two vessels eventually stopped in what is now Vancouver Island in 1778, and the crew traded with the local Yuquot people. While hospitable, the Yuquot were more demanding of the visitors than the previous natives Cook had encountered and desired metal items rather than the usual trinkets that Cook and his men would give.

Cook continued his voyage north, traveling up the Canadian and Alaskan coastlines and eventually located the Bering Strait. This is why Cook Inlet is so named in this area in Alaska. Cook then traveled across the Strait to Russia, realizing that they were now at the easternmost tip of Asia.

The trip failed to discover a Northwest Passage that could sail around North America, but they did confirm that North America and Asia were almost connected. The only reason Cook was not able to continue to travel north into the Arctic was that the ice blocked his route.

The men were exhausted as well and desired to return to warmer weather. Cook elected to take the ships south to

Hawaii to explore there. The two ships spent two months sailing around the islands and mapping them before making landfall on Hawaii Island.

When Cook and his men landed in Hawaii, a major Hawaiian harvest festival called Makahiki was going on. This festival was to worship the Polynesian fertility and agriculture god Lono.

By sheer coincidence, Cook's two ships resembled objects and artifacts that were worshiped by the Hawaiians for Lono. By yet another coincidence, Cook's clockwise route around Hawaii paralleled the clockwise processions that took place around the island..., and the Hawaiians had observed Cook's ships from the shore.

For these reasons, the Hawaiians initially believed that Cook was either Lono incarnated, or someone deified and sent by Lono. Cook and his men were subsequently greeted very warmly by the Hawaiians when they came ashore.

Cook decided to stay in Hawaii for a month so his men could recuperate and enjoy themselves. After the month was up, Cook and his men set sail again to continue their exploration of the Pacific, but they were forced to return when the foremast of the *Resolution* broke.

This time, Cook and his men were not greeted so warmly by the Hawaiians. Cook led the two ships into Kealakekua Bay, intending to use wood from the forests to make a new mast. While Cook and his men were repairing the Resolution, native Hawaiians secretly stole one of the longboats. More native warriors later appeared and threatened to attack the men as well. The Hawaiians were starting to figure out that Cook was not, in fact, their god Lono.

Enraged, Cook resolved to capture the King of Hawaii, Kalani'opu'u, and hold him for ransom. On February 14, 1779, Cook and his men marched armed into the village intending to grab the King and hold him hostage to get their longboat back.

Realizing Cook's intentions, a crowd of native Hawaiians surrounded him and his men and blocked their route. Realizing that the Hawaiians were about to become hostile and weren't going to let them seize the King without a fight, Cook and his men turned back around and started walking back to the boats on the shore, intending to row back to the ship.

Suddenly, the natives attacked with clubs and bladed weapons. Cook suffered a blow from a club to his head, and when he landed in the water along the shore, he was also stabbed numerous times by the natives.

A fight then broke out for Cook's body, with the Hawaiians winning and dragging it back toward their village. Four of Cook's men were killed and two more were wounded during the fight.

The Hawaiians later disemboweled Cook's body, burned the flesh from his bones, and cleaned and preserved his bones. Some of these bones were then sent to his crew so he could be buried at sea.

In 1780, the expedition returned home, but this time Cook was only with them in spirit.

****

Cook spent a grand total of 12 years sailing around the world. Because of his efforts, Europeans greatly expanded their knowledge of the islands of the Pacific Ocean, Australia, New Zealand, Newfoundland, North America, and even Antarctica. Antarctica was confirmed as the lost seventh continent, and Cook proved that North America and Asia are closely linked via Alaska and Russia.

Cook's maps were renowned for being extremely precise. Not only was Cook very talented at mapmaking, but he was also skilled at accurately calculating the position of his latitude and longitude.

More than 3,000 new species of plants and animals were catalogued on Cook's voyages as well, greatly increasing humanity's scientific knowledge.

Cook was widely respected throughout the world during his lifetime as well, so much so that even when hostilities broke out between the American colonies and Great Britain in the Revolutionary War, the American naval vessels were ordered not to engage Cook's vessel should they come into contact with it.

Cook greatly increased our knowledge of the world at sea. Less than a hundred years after his time, another famed British explorer would contribute to European knowledge of the world on land, and specifically of the African interior. His name was David Livingstone.

DAVID LIVINGSTONE'S SEARCH FOR THE SOURCE OF THE NILE

Missionary and abolitionist Dr. David Livingstone embarked on a four-year journey throughout Africa in an obsessive quest to find the source of the Nile River. In the process, he named Victoria Falls, crossed the width of southern Africa, and helped bring an end to the Arab-Swahili slave trade.

David Livingstone was a famous and almost mythic British missionary and abolitionist who explored not because of a thirst for adventure or a desire for riches. Rather, Livingstone sought to bring an absolute end to the Arab-Swahili slave trade.

Livingstone believed that by finding the source of the Nile River, which at that time was unknown, he could use his influence to help end the slave trade that was going on in that area.

While much of Africa had been explored and colonized by the mid-1800s, there were also vast areas of the interior of the continent that were completely unexplored by Europeans. This area of Africa was commonly referred to as the "dark interior," reflecting Europeans' lack of knowledge and fear of what lurked there. Livingstone would prove instrumental in the European exploration of this region.

****

Livingstone was born on March 19, 1813, in Blantyre, Scotland. He was born in a tenement building for workers of a cotton factory. From the age of ten, Livingstone worked in the cotton factory as a cotton piercer, commonly putting in 12-hour days. The money Livingstone made was used to help provide for his family.

Livingstone's father, Neil, was a devout Christian, a Sunday school teacher, and a recovering alcoholic. Making a living as a tea salesman who went door-to-door, Neil was well-read on both travel and theology and taught much of what he knew to his children. Even though Livingstone worked long hours from his youth, that didn't stop him from learning much about Christianity and the world from his father.

In his spare time, Livingstone enjoyed going outdoors to collect plant and animal specimens. Livingstone had an intense interest in science and the natural world, and he believed that both religion and science could be easily reconciled together.

Besides the influence of his father, Livingstone received his education from a local village school attended by the children of other cotton mill families. Livingstone then traveled to Anderson's University in Glasgow to study medicine and chemistry. He attended anti-slavery lectures while he was in school as well, which left a major impression on him for the rest of his life.

The next major turning point in Livingstone's life was in 1840 when he set sail as a missionary to the Cape of Good Hope. He studied the Tswana and Dutch languages during the journey to help prepare himself for his stay in Africa. The captain of the ship Livingstone was on taught him critical navigational skills as well.

En route to the Cape of Good Hope, the ship made a stop in Rio de Janeiro. Livingstone was impressed by the architecture of the buildings there and ministered to drunken American and British sailors he encountered.

From there, the ship carried onto South Africa, finally arriving at Simon's Bay in March 1841. Livingstone firmly believed that all men were created equal before God and that this applied to the British, the Dutch settlers, and the local African tribes. This put him at odds with many of the people he met there.

Livingstone spent several months embarking on long treks into the African interior, heading north into what is now Botswana with other missionaries.

Once, he was attacked by a lion while defending sheep. Despite managing to shoot the animal, he was reloading when it got back on its feet and attacked him, knocking him to the ground and biting and breaking his left arm. Livingstone was only saved because another man shot the lion while it was mauling him.

Thankfully, Livingstone's arm healed quickly, and he regained his strength by lifting weights. However, he would not be able to lift the left arm above his shoulder for the rest of his life. Livingstone married the woman who tended to his injuries, Mary, in January 1845.

****

Livingstone continued his missionary work in southern Africa for many years. He sought to set up more mission stations, even if this meant traveling north into the so-called "dark interior" of Africa if necessary. In 1849, Livingstone set out on an expedition with some companions across the Kalahari Desert, eventually reaching Lake Ngami in northern Botswana and then the Zambezi River.

The Zambezi River was widely regarded as the gateway into the "dark interior" - or the point at which most Europeans who traveled that far into Africa stopped. The chief of a local tribe on the Zambezi allowed Livingstone to set up a trading post along the river and even provided warriors who were to serve as interpreters and guides.

Livingstone spent the next several years finding suitable trade routes between the Zambezi River and the coast, coming into contact with the Portuguese but nearly dying from fever in the process. During these journeys, Livingstone gave Victoria Falls their English name (for Queen Victoria). The natives called the falls the Mosi-oa-Tunya (Thundering Smoke).

Livingstone was able to map the entire Zambezi River and find a suitable route for crossing Africa from the Atlantic Ocean on one side to the Indian Ocean on the other. He became the first European to successfully cross Africa at that approximate latitude, and the trade routes that he established were successfully used by the British, Portuguese, and Arab traders, among others.

****

While Livingstone was a proponent of using the trade routes he charted and mapped for their intended purpose, he also developed the primary goal of abolishing the slave trade altogether. He coined the motto "Christianity. Commerce, and Civilization," which is inscribed on his statue at Victoria Falls to this day.

Finally returning to his native Great Britain in the mid-1850s, Livingstone was awarded the Patron's Medal by the Royal Geographical Society for his work in establishing a suitable trade route across Africa. He also was accepted into the Royal Society and was in great demand as a public speaker, since people wanted to know about what he had seen in Africa.

Livingstone was encouraged to run more expeditions in Africa to establish more commercial trade routes, but he primarily wanted to use the trade routes to displace the slave trade.

The British Foreign Office proposed that Livingstone lead a second expedition along the Zambezi River. Tragically, Livingstone's wife Mary contracted malaria and passed away on this expedition. Nonetheless, despite being devastated by the loss of his wife, Livingstone completed the expedition via steamer ship.

Livingstone then traveled to Zanzibar, an island off the coast of Tanzania. His new obsession was to locate the source of the Nile River. It was generally believed that either Lake Victoria or Lake Albert was the source, but there was still great debate over the issue. Livingstone was of the differing opinion that the real source of the Nile was further south than believed. He put together a team of freed African slaves and Indians to lead an expedition to find out once and for all.

Livingstone had a motive beyond knowledge. He believed if he could locate the source of his Nile, he could use his resulting reputation to gain the necessary clout to successfully end the African-Arab slave trade.

The expedition set out from the Ruvuma River, but to Livingstone's dismay, several of the men who had initially joined the expedition began to desert him. In fact, some of the men who left him returned to the authorities in

Zanzibar and claimed that Livingstone had died, even though that wasn't true!

Livingstone and what remained of his expedition came to Lake Malawi in August. Despite running low on supplies and his health increasingly declining, Livingstone nonetheless pressed on, venturing onward with slave traders to Lake Mweru, Lake Bangweulu, and the Lualaba River.

In 1869, while exploring the African jungle, Livingstone became stricken with pneumonia and cholera. Ironically enough, Livingstone's life was saved by Arab slave traders who discovered him and gave him the medications that he needed to stay alive.

While recovering, however, Livingstone witnessed a brutal massacre of over 400 Africans at the hands of the slave traders. Watching the incident devastated Livingstone to the same extent that the passing of his wife Mary had, and he lost his desire to continue searching for the source of the Nile River.

Despite still being in ill health, he managed to travel back the way he came. Livingstone eventually came to an Arabian settlement on the coast of Lake Tanganyika. Even though he had failed to find the source of the Nile River, he had succeeded in locating numerous lakes and geographical features of the African interior that had been unknown to Europeans up until that time.

Another British explorer, Henry Morton Stanley, had been dispatched to find Livingstone, who could have easily been dead as far as the authorities knew. Stanley discovered Livingstone at the Arabian settlement and - according to most versions of the tale - uttered the famous words, "Dr. Livingstone, I presume?" to which Livingstone replied, "I feel thankful that I am here to welcome you." This statement may be a myth as it cannot be verified.

Despite his health failing, Livingstone spent the last several years of his life in Africa continuing to explore the interior. He passed away in 1873 at the age of 60, in present-day Zambia, from internal bleeding and malaria.

After this death, Livingstone's heart was removed from his body and placed under a tree near where he died.

****

The exploits of Livingstone were critical to increasing European awareness about the tribes and geography of the interior of Africa. Perhaps more importantly, the public writings he composed did much to stir the public against the slave trade. His work opened up the African interior to missionaries who followed his same routes and preached to the African tribes residing within those lands.

Livingstone was widely respected among African tribes because he treated them with kindness and respect, even if they did not convert to Christianity. Livingstone envisioned an Africa where Christian European colonists could co-exist with the African tribes without slavery.

Today, David Livingstone is regarded as one of the most influential British missionaries and explorers of all time.

ROBERT PEARY'S POLAR EXPEDITIONS

American naval officer Robert Peary was bound and determined to become the first American to travel the furthest north. While some controversy remains concerning whether he really did reach the North Pole, there's no question that Peary became one of the most fearless and important explorers of the Arctic.

In the early 1900s, it was known that Earth was round, which meant that it was only logical that both a North and a South Pole existed on opposite ends of the planet. Getting there, however, was a different story.

The world was shrinking. Much of Earth had been navigated since the days of Columbus and Magellan. Ships were now traveling the seas all over the globe and much of the interior land masses of South America, Africa, and Asia had been explored by Europeans as well.

Two areas of the Earth had yet to be discovered by any (modern) human and continued to capture imaginations:

the North and the South Pole. Both were (and still are) among the most mysterious places on Earth. They're also both extremely dangerous, being surrounded by sheer ice and freezing winds.

The North Pole is also vastly different from the South Pole. Antarctica is a land mass and even contains human relics, suggesting that ancient human civilizations may have inhabited the area when it was not an icy wasteland like it is today.

But the North Pole has no landmasses at all. The land that comes closest is from Canada and Greenland. This means that explorers who venture that far north have to travel directly over ice, in extremely frigid temperatures. The North Pole is simply one of the most inhospitable regions on Earth, and many ships that travel that far north become trapped in the ice, making travel there a dangerous gamble.

This is why explorers who have traveled to the North Pole usually take a ship as far as they can safely do so before disembarking and traveling on foot and sled. This is how one adventurer, Robert Peary, reached the North Pole.

Peary made no less than eight attempts to reach the North Pole during his adventures in the Arctic Circle. The first seven attempts failed, but in September 1909, headlines all over the world announced that Peary had finally reached the North Pole on his eighth attempt!

Peary was quickly celebrated and compared to the likes of Christopher Columbus for his feat.

But then other headlines started being run that another man, Frederick Cook, had discovered the North Pole before Peary. In fact, there were headlines in the *New York Herald* about Cook's discovery a full week before the headlines about Peary; the news of Peary's achievement had just reached more newspapers and thus made the news on a larger scale first.

The big question then became: Who was the *first* to reach the North Pole?

****

Robert Peary was born on May 6, 1856, in Pennsylvania. In his youth, Peary worked as a profile surveyor in Maine. He would climb to the top of Jockey Cap Rock in Fryeburg and create maps and surveys of the mountains and hills that he could see from the summit. He also worked as a draftsman for the United States National Geodetic Survey, gaining more experience in surveying and mapmaking.

In 1881, Peary enlisted in the United States Navy and served as an engineer, creating more maps and surveys in Nicaragua. For reasons that no one knows, Peary became obsessed during his time in the Navy with becoming the first man to reach the North Pole. We know this from a diary entry he made in 1885.

A year later, he published papers in the National Academy of Sciences explaining methods he believed could be used to cross Greenland's ice cap to reach the North Pole. He also proposed the strategy of starting from Baffin Island rather than Greenland.

Even though Peary failed in his first seven attempts to reach the North Pole, with each attempt he and his team learned more about the unpredictable nature of the ice and which routes wouldn't work.

Frederick Cook was a member of one of Peary's expeditions. Cook was another explorer who sought fame, and after returning from an expedition with Peary, he resolved to undertake an expedition of his own rather than fall under Peary's shadow.

Cook was ambitious and sought recognition for other exploits as well. For example, he claimed he was the first man to climb to the summit of Mount Denali in Alaska.

After Peary returned from his eighth (and first successful) expedition into the Arctic, it didn't take long for him to hear the news that Cook had already reached the North Pole around a week before him.

Peary immediately went to work to expose Cook for having lied and to secure his claim to having reached the North Pole first. Cook had provided many journal entries explaining descriptions of the North Pole as well as photographs to prove his claims.

Peary's claim, meanwhile, rested on the idea that he was the only man who possessed the knowledge to reach the North Pole based on his reputation as an avid Arctic explorer. He argued that there was no possible way Cook had the knowledge to reach the North Pole.

Peary stated that he had made multiple attempts before finding a suitable route to the North Pole. Cook had only joined one of his expeditions (the second out of the eight) and therefore couldn't have possibly known how to find a route through the icy terrain so quickly.

****

The dispute between the two men eventually reached the United States House of Representatives in 1911. The House interviewed members of both expeditions and also carefully analyzed the journal entries and the photographs that Cook had provided.

Based on its findings, the House came to a different conclusion: neither Peary nor Cook had reached the North Pole first.

That's because a member of Peary's party, Matthew Henson, reached the North Pole first! Here's what the Committee said happened according to its findings. When Peary was closing in on the general vicinity of the Pole, he sent Henson up ahead to scout the land. Henson would have therefore reached the North Pole first before Peary and the rest of his team arrived!

Cook's account was also found to be rife with issues. It is known that Cook returned to the Arctic in 1907 following his expedition to Mt. Denali. He reached northern Greenland in February 1908 before setting out with a party of two Intuits. The three men were gone for about 14 months, but where they went exactly remains controversial. The validity of Cook's alleged description and photos of the North Pole were deemed unprovable.

Part of the problem is that Cook never produced navigational records to prove he had reached the North Pole, and the sextant navigational data he showed later was found to have inaccurate data (the solar diameter was incorrect).

Plus, Cook's photos that he claimed showed his ascent to the top of Mt. Denali proved to be of a shorter peak. That dealt a blow to his reputation, as did an ongoing campaign by Peary and his team to discredit Cook.

That's why, to this day, Peary is widely taught in the history books as having been the first man recorded to reach the North Pole. Whether he was the first is a debate that continues to rage, similar to debates about whether Christopher Columbus was really the first European to reach the Americas.

****

The North Pole remains clouded in mystery a century after the Peary and Cook expeditions.

Richard Byrd, an American explorer and Naval officer who also became famous for exploring Antarctica, claims that he took off from northern Norway in a plane in 1926 in an attempt to find the North Pole. But like Cook, the data he produced concerning the North Pole was shown to be slightly inaccurate in terms of his coordinates, indicating that he may not have reached the North Pole after all.

Some people even claim that the true existence of the North Pole has never been proven or at least not released to the public. Proponents of the Hollow Earth theory, for instance, contend that the real North Pole contains an entranceway into the interior of the Earth, which is where many mythologies supposedly come from. Others claim that the Hollow Earth theory is complete hogwash and inaccurate as well.

Regardless of what lies at the North Pole, the Pole at the opposite end of the world is equally mysterious. Just like the North Pole, people often try to imagine what setting foot at the South Pole would be like - and, in fact, Antarctica as a whole.

Almost as equally inhospitable as the North Pole, the South Pole and the surrounding Antarctic landmass have stopped many expeditions cold in their tracks and forced their members to face a tough fight just to live.

One of these expeditions was led by Ernest Shackleton.

ERNEST SHACKLETON'S BATTLE FOR SURVIVAL IN ANTARCTICA

One of the most well-known figures of what became known as the Heroic Age of Antarctic Exploration, Ernest Shackleton was a pioneer of exploring the Earth's southernmost continent. As war broke out across Europe in 1914, Shackleton and his crew waged their own war for survival while being stranded for more than two years in Antarctica.

Ernest Shackleton is perhaps the most famous explorer of Antarctica of all time. He led no less than three expeditions to the Antarctic region and faced treacherous conditions and many dangerous scenarios throughout.

Born in Ireland on February 15, 1874, Shackleton began taking part in British explorations of polar regions when he joined the Discovery expedition from 1901–1904. Later, he joined the Nimrod expedition of 1907–1909, which took him to less than 200 miles from the South Pole. The South Pole was later reached by Roald Amundsen in 1911.

Nonetheless, vast regions of Antarctica remained unexplored.

While Amundsen may have secured recognition as the first to reach the South Pole, Shackleton wanted acclaim for a different kind of Antarctic endeavor: He wanted to become the first person to lead an expedition from one side of Antarctica to the other.

This became known as the Imperial Trans-Antarctica Expedition. When this expedition was launched, only ten men had ever reached the South Pole, and five of those men had been killed trying to return. Shackleton wanted to cross from one side of Antarctica to the other, and he specifically wanted to cross through the South Pole to do it.

Needless to say, Shackleton was about to find himself in one of the most harrowing battles for survival in recorded history—but not the one he might have expected.

****

As it would turn out, the men who embarked on the Imperial Trans-Antarctica Expedition would never even get to set foot on continental Antarctica.

Shackleton began planning the journey in earnest in 1909 after he had returned from the Nimrod expedition. He planned to leave from the Weddell Sea at the southern tip of South America, and then cross an unexplored region of Antarctica before ending up in New Zealand on the opposite side.

The ship to be used for the journey was *Endurance*, which was built in Norway and was originally intended to be used for Arctic tourist cruises. When Shackleton's expedition formally launched after he secured funding, World War I had broken out in Europe. Shackleton offered to give up the expedition and provide *Endurance* to the war effort, but the British government told him to proceed with the expedition anyway.

Endurance then set sail for Antarctica from Buenos Aires with 28 men aboard. It turned out to be a particularly ice-heavy year, and so *Endurance* was forced to stop at South Georgia further from the coastline of southern South America. During their stay, the men from the ship formed friendships with the Norwegian whalers who were also stationed there.

When the ice had broken up enough to sail, *Endurance* set sail again with extra coal in her stores. This coal was crucial to push through the thousand miles of pack ice in the Weddell Sea. It took *Endurance* six weeks to do so.

The ship was within 100 miles of its destination when disaster struck. The ice had become so thick that *Endurance* was unable to push through.

On January 18, 1915, the ice completely encased all sides of the ship.

Endurance - and Shackleton and his men - was stuck!

****

Even though Shackleton was greatly disappointed by this turn of events, his men respected and looked up to him, referring to him as "The Boss." Therefore, Shackleton knew he had to display confidence and decisiveness in his actions to maintain this respect from his men, and more importantly, to save their lives.

As the ice drifted in a southwest direction, *Endurance* drifted with it. The men worked hard to free the ship, but whenever cracks appeared in the ice, they were forced to disengage from the effort. The ice continued drifting and took the ship with it.

By February, it was clear that the ship was stuck at sub-zero temperatures and the men would be trapped there for the winter. The chief concern was now where the drifting ice would take them...

The Antarctic winter set in, which meant long and especially dark nights. The men played football and hockey over the ice to help pass the time. They could only hope that the ice would break up and *Endurance* would be able to escape.

Months passed. By July, the sun and daylight began to return, but along with them came brutal blizzards that forced the men to spend most of their time in shelters struggling for warmth. Shackleton and his men knew that if the ice did not break up to free *Endurance*, the vessel would instead become crushed by the ice.

When their food supplies began running low, the men started hunting for seals and penguins to provide meat for themselves and the dogs. They had drifted nearly 12,000 miles and were now about 350 miles from Paulet Island, the closest port where there would be food, water, and rescue.

Then further disaster struck as the men's worst fears were realized.

****

In October 1915, the ice began to crush *Endurance*. The stern post became twisted, and a hole was punctured in the ship. The men climbed aboard and ran water pumps to get the water out.

But Shackleton knew that the ship was doomed. He ordered all food, supplies, and lifeboats to be removed from it and set up in a camp on the ice. This camp became known as "Ocean Camp."

Finally, on November 21, 1915, *Endurance* broke from the ice and sank below the waters. Thankfully, the men had rescued most of the supplies and gear onboard.

Still, the men were stranded with no communication methods with the outside world and dwindling supplies.

To make matters worse, the Antarctic Spring had struck, and the ice was finally starting to break up. If *Endurance* was still afloat this would have been great news, but now it meant that the men had to constantly be on guard. The ground below their feet could break up at any moment!

Shackleton decided that the time had come to leave the camp and begin a search for dry land, hopefully near Paulet

Island. The men had three lifeboats and were able to haul two of them - *James Caird* and *Dudley Docker*. The third lifeboat, *Stancomb Wills*, was abandoned. The boats were around 20 feet long.

In the Spring of 1916, the men began to journey across Antarctica. They would either carry the boats over the ice or if the ice became too thin, they would climb into the boats and make their way over open water.

The men continued for months in this manner, but because of the drifting sea ice, they were only able to travel 30 miles from their original location.

Eventually, they reached Elephant Island. It was the first dry land that they had set foot on in *years*. They made a camp and called it "Point Wild."

Shackleton knew that there was no hope of rescue because they had sighted no ships passing through the area. As a result, Shackleton decided that the only hope of rescue was to send out a lifeboat with men to the nearest area with people, which was a whaling station in South Georgia over 800 miles away.

The journey would be harrowing. There would be 50-foot waves in the ocean enroute. The men who embarked on the boat would also have to navigate using the sun.

Shackleton left one of the men, Frank Wild, to command the men on Elephant Island. He informed them that if no rescue came by Spring, then they could make for Deception Island, which was known to be visited by whalers.

Shackleton set off in *James Caird* with five other men on April 24, 1916, with the other men remaining back in the other lifeboat that they had converted into a hut.

Shackleton and his crew were able to make fairly good progress despite the small size of the vessel and the rough seas. They managed to cover up to 70 miles per day. The men were always freezing and soaked to the skin because water would spray over the sides of the boat and render their clothing, blankets, and sleeping bags wet.

Ice would also accumulate on the boat, sometimes up to more than a foot thick, forcing the men to use improvised tools to chip away at it. The ice forming was a danger because it weighed down the boat. The men's fingers and hands became afflicted with frostbite.

Finally, after about a week, sunshine broke out and provided much-needed warmth to the men. They were also able to calculate that they were more than halfway to their goal of South Georgia. The ice began to become less of an issue as well.

The air started to become warmer, and the men caught sight of sea birds, which told them that they were closer to getting to dry land. Finally, the men caught sight of South Georgia, exactly two weeks after they had departed from Elephant Island.

****

The men had to overcome reefs, high winds, and shallow rocks along the coast to reach dry land. It took multiple attempts and over a day before they were finally able to get into a cove.

But now Shackleton and the five other men were in an entirely new situation. Even though they had reached South Georgia island and were standing on land, they had to trek more than 20 miles over glaciers and rocky and mountainous terrain to the nearest whaling station.

After several days of hiking up and down this kind of terrain (which involved rappelling down rocky terrains), they caught sight of a whaling boat entering a bay. The men had to climb down a waterfall - becoming soaked to the skin in the process - before they finally made it down to the bottom and arrived at the Stromness whaling station.

The men were exhausted, with matted long hair and tattered clothes, but they were alive.

Shackleton immediately got to work with the local authorities to rescue the 22 men who were still trapped on Elephant Island. They initially took off in a British whaling ship called *Southern Sky*, but it was unable to push through the pack ice. The men had to retreat to the Falkland Islands, where they were loaded onto another ship from the Uruguayan government.

When this ship also failed to get through the ice, the men chartered yet another ship called *Emma*, but when the engine on this ship broke as well, the men were forced to try a fourth vessel. They were loaned a steam tug called *Yelcho* from the Chilean government, which was able to push through the ice and reach Elephant Island by August 30, 1916. The men were rescued!

****

Remarkably, *not one man* in Shackleton's crew was lost. The *James Caird* boat was preserved and remains in England to this day.

Even though Shackleton may not have succeeded in his mission to cross the Antarctic, he displayed incredible leadership skills in keeping his men together and ensuring that no one was killed. The survival of Shackleton and his men for two years in Antarctica is one of the most incredible real-life stories of survival.

Shackleton wasn't finished with visiting Antarctica either; at least, not in his mind. In 1921, he wanted to return to Antarctica to map out the coastline, but enroute to the continent, he succumbed to a heart attack at the age of 47.

Shackleton's death marked the end of the period known as the Heroic Age of Antarctic Exploration…, but not to the age of exploration as a whole.

RANULPH FIENNES: THE WORLD'S GREATEST LIVING EXPLORER

Known as 'the world's greatest living explorer, 'Ranulph Fiennes became the first person to completely cross Antarctica on foot. Plus, despite suffering from several serious health issues, Fiennes ascended Everest, crossed both ice caps, and completed seven marathons in seven days across seven continents.

Some people probably will tell you that the Age of Exploration is long gone. But Ranulph Fiennes would probably tell you that the age of exploration and adventure is far from over.

A veteran of the British army who served in counter-insurgency service missions, Fiennes is one of the most accomplished explorers and adventurers to this day.

Fiennes is notable for a range of accomplishments. He visited both the North Pole and the South Pole and became the first person to completely cross Antarctica from one end to the other on foot. And at the age of 65, he followed that up by ascending Mt. Everest.

****

Fiennes was born on March 7, 1944. After World War II concluded, Fiennes's mother moved the family to South Africa, where he lived until the age of 12. He then returned to England in his teenage years and was formally educated at Sandroyd School and Eton College.

Fiennes then enlisted in the Mons Officer Cadet School and was commissioned to serve in the Royal Scots Greys, the same unit in which his father had served. Fiennes served in the British military until 1971.

Fiennes had been going on expeditions since 1961, however. Most notably, he led a hovercraft up the Nile River in 1969 and on glaciers in Norway in 1970.

Perhaps his most astonishing expedition was in 1979 when Fiennes undertook the Transglobe Expedition. He and two other friends traveled the entire world on its polar axis, which no one has accomplished since. In doing so, he also completed the Northwest Passage, the sea lane located through the Arctic Ocean in between the Pacific and the Atlantic oceans.

It's not just adventures on which Fiennes has embarked. He has contributed massively to modern-day exploration as well. In 1992, he commanded an expedition that located the lost city of Iram in Oman. Iram is a fabled lost city that is mentioned in the Quran but was believed by many to not have existed in real life. Fiennes' expedition helped to prove otherwise.

In 2000, Fiennes attempted to reach the North Pole on foot, but his plan was foiled when his sled broke through the ice. Although Fiennes was able to pull the sled out with his hands, he suffered severe frostbite in the process. He was later forced to amputate the ends of his frostbitten fingers, which Fiennes did himself using an electric foresaw.

Despite the loss of the ends of his fingers and suffering from a heart attack after that, Fiennes continued to live his adventurous lifestyle. He completed seven marathons in seven days on seven continents in an event that became known as the Land Rover 7x7x7 Challenge. Fiennes raced the seven marathons in Patagonia, Antarctica, Australia, Asia, Europe, Africa, and North America.

In May 2009, after multiple failed attempts, Fiennes became the oldest British person to ascend to the top of Mt. Everest.

****

Fiennes's entire life story is a testament to one crucial and yet commonly overlooked fact: There is still so much more of the world to explore and so many adventures to go on.

Many people, in the hustle and bustle of everyday life, may be under the false impression that all of the world has been explored and that there's nowhere else to go.

Nothing could be further from the truth.

That's because there are still many areas of the world that have yet to be explored. Did you know that much of the Amazon Rainforest remains unexplored? That's because certain areas of the rainforest remain inaccessible to this day.

Likewise, parts of the vast and sprawling Sahara Desert in northern Africa are unexplored as well. The same is true for the depths of the jungles of the Congo Basin in Central Africa. Many areas of Antarctica remain completely untouched by humans too.

Fiennes may be considered the world's greatest living explorer by the *Guiness Book of World Records*, but he certainly won't be the last. The above areas of the world still need to be explored, and it will only be a matter of time before they are.

CONCLUSION

We've now arrived at the end of a long journey.

In the vast and ever-changing events of human history, exploration has been a defining thread, woven throughout each age. From the earliest intrepid voyages from ancient civilizations across uncharted waters to the bold journeys into the unexplored realms of continents, the spirit of exploration has driven us to venture into the unknown, to seek knowledge and understanding, and to discover the wonders and mysteries that lie beyond the familiar horizons of our everyday lives.

Within the page of this book, we have covered the stories of intrepid explorers who dared to challenge the limits of their time and circumstances.

Marco Polo ventured deep into the Asian interior to establish a partnership (and later a friendship) with Kublai Khan. In the process, he helped set the foundation for an understanding between West and East.

Vasco da Gama found a seafaring route around the southern tip of Africa to India, proving to Europeans that Asia and Europe could be connected via ship and not just by land.

Ferdinand Magellan set sail from Europe to completely circumnavigate the world, proving that it could be done and sacrificing his life in the process.

Christopher Columbus made it to the New World to essentially begin the modern age in which there is an unbreakable relationship between America and Europe. Further research into his life hints that there was more to European knowledge of the Americas than meets the eye—leaving us more ideas to explore.

Amerigo Vespucci ventured to the Americas as well, and in the process, his name and life story lent further credence to the idea that the Americas may have already been known to certain Europeans, completely changing the way we view history as a result.

Francisco Pizarro sailed through Panama to reach South America from the west, and with just a few dozen men, he was able to conquer an entire empire and completely change the entire history of South America.

James Cook developed maps of multiple regions of the world, including Antarctica and vast swaths of the Pacific and its islands, that were amazingly accurate and still in use into the 1900s. We owe much of what we know about the world to Cook.

David Livingstone bravely ventured deep into the heart of Africa and discovered routes to travel from one end of the continent to the other to end the African-Arab slave trade, a worthy and difficult task.

Robert Peary went further north than anyone had likely gone before him to bring the world its first news of the North Pole. That was only around a hundred years ago!

Ernest Shackleton proved through sheer resilience and strength that people can survive in the most inhospitable places on Earth for great periods. The feat of Shackleton and his men to survive for over two years in Antarctica remains unparalleled even to this day.

Through the triumphs and struggles of these men, we have witnessed the resilience of the human spirit and the unyielding pursuit of knowledge and discovery. They have taught us that exploration is not merely about conquering new frontiers, but also about overcoming personal barriers, embracing diversity, and fostering a deeper connection with our world and its inhabitants.

As we reach the conclusion of this journey, one truth becomes apparent. As Ranulph Fiennes has clearly proven to us, exploration is not a series of events of the past. Rather, it is an eternal flame that burns within each of us. The spirit of exploration lives on, beckoning us to cast off the shackles of complacency and to venture forth into the unexplored territories of the world and discover new science, art, and culture from lost or forgotten civilizations as a result.

Our world today stands at the edge of new frontiers, awaiting the bold and visionary minds who will rise to the call of exploration. In the face of unprecedented challenges, from environmental crises to technological revolutions, the lessons of our explorer ancestors offer guidance and inspiration.

As we close this book, try to remember that the journey of exploration is never truly finished. It is a continuing and ongoing event, an ever-evolving story that we all have the power to shape.

There are also many more explorers and adventurers that we weren't able to cover in this book. To continue your research, be sure to read up on names like Hernan Cortes, Jeanne Baret, John Cabot, Henry Hudson, Amelia Earhart, and Francis Drake, among others.

If you were an explorer living today in the modern age, where would you go?

Printed in Great Britain
by Amazon

36655690R00089